How to respond to a ske?tic

How to respond to a skeptic

Lewis A. Drummond
Paul R. Baxter

MOODY PRESS
CHICAGO

© 1986 by

THE MOODY BIBLE INSTITUTE
OF CHICAGO

All Scripture quotations, unless noted otherwise, are from the *New
American Standard Bible,* © 1960, 1962, 1963, 1968, 1971, 1972, 1973,
1975, and 1977 by the Lockman Foundation, and are used by
permission.

Library of Congress Cataloging-in Publication Data

Drummond, Lewis A.
    How to respond to a skeptic.

    1. Apologetics—20th century .   2. Skepticism.
I. Baxter, Paul R., 1947—   .   II. Title.
BT1211.D78   1986   239   85-28476
ISBN 0-8024-7703-8 (pbk.)

1 2 3 4 5 6   Printing/GT/Year   90 89 88 87 86

Printed in the United States of America

Contents

Preface

The Bible makes it crystal clear: Christians are to witness for Jesus Christ. Our Lord said, "You shall be My witnesses" (Acts 1:8). But speaking of Christ is not always comfortable, especially when one meets a skeptic who has serious doubts, problems, and quite plausible arguments as to why he rejects faith in the Lord Jesus Christ. To speak of our faith with one predisposed to listen, one with an open, seeking mind, is not too difficult, but the skeptic is another matter. Yet, we can not escape or evade the call to communicate Christ to the critic. The Bible says, "Always being ready to make a defense to *everyone* who asks you to give an account for the hope that is in you" (1 Peter 3:15, italics added). We must be prepared to witness, even to the doubting skeptic.

That unavoidable assignment is formidable. How can one "always be ready"? We need some resources. Furthermore, we are attempting to live out our faith in an increasingly skeptical age. The need for aid in sharing Christ intelligently and convincingly is vital if we are to point others to faith in the Lord. This small volume is designed to help do just that.

It is important to realize that the arguments and the analyses of the various thinkers are presented in mere outline form. No attempt has been made to give an exhaustive analysis of the various views and personalities. They are intended only to provide a vehicle for the various skeptical views. This book is not a technically philosophical work. No attempt has been made to be exhaustive. A full volume could — and perhaps should — be written on each chapter.

The approach here is simple — but we hope not simplistic. The purpose is to present in capsule form some sensible and convincing reasons for believing that it is intelligent and wise to receive Christ as Lord and Savior. Christians need answers for the doubter and skeptic if we are to help him find Christ. We must never lose sight of that goal: To lead others to Christ. The love of Christ is to be our constraining motive.

We may also find some answers to our own problems with our faith. We have times of doubting too, and this may provide help in a moment of need.

Furthermore, there is a special form of doubt and skepticism that is found among the so-called "disenfranchised." This root of skepticism grows in people who feel that organized Christianity has socially failed them. It is found in the ghettos and slums of our cities. This book of limited space and scope cannot deal with the situation in all its social ramifications. But it may alert us to be sensitive to those who are caught in the trap of the ghetto mentally.

Gratitude must be expressed to those who contributed to this book's production. The typists at Southern Baptist Theological Seminary and Mrs. Lewis A. Drummond and Mrs. Paul R. Baxter, who proofread the manuscript, all did an excellent job. Thus it goes forth with the prayer that we may be "ready to make a defense" — ready to witness for Christ positively, joyfully, and effectively.

1

Responding to a Skeptic: The Why and How

In a university philosophy class, a mismatched debate erupted between the professor and a freshman. The professor had been lecturing for several days on various world religions. In this particular discourse, Christianity became the topic. He made it clear he was not a believing Christian as he spiced up his lecture with irreverent jokes and sarcastic comments about the Christian position.

Most of the students laughed at the professor's clever and caustic comments about what he called the "myth of faith." Even though I was a Christian and something of a trained debater, I offered no defense. I simply sat and listened transfixed, perhaps a little chagrined, by the professor's sophisticated and pungent oratory. Suddenly, however, a freshman girl in the class surprised us all. Although she had said absolutely nothing during the previous six weeks of class discussion, this day she dramatically broke her silence and triggered a confrontation with the professor by asking him a simple yet quite profound question: "Why are you so biased against the Christian religion?"

The professor, noticeably startled by her blunt, forthright question, paused for a moment. He then replied in a courteous but slightly condescending manner, "Well, as far as I can tell, Christianity and all religions are nothing but mythological, illogical philosophies that are beyond belief."

Perhaps he thought that would end the conversation, but the girl pressed on undaunted. In a calm yet passionate voice she said, "What I believe may seem foolish to you, but to me it is far more true than anything I have heard or read in this class."

"OK," the professor responded, "let's talk about your faith." It resulted in a question and answer period of unusual intensity on the part of the combatants and unusual interest on the part of the class.

The professor sat down on his desk and posed the question, "Do you really believe in someone you cannot see? If so, surely you realize that you are not being scientific but simply superstitious?"

The student answered immediately, "Can you deny that the wind is real? Can you see the wind? You believe it is real because you feel its effect. Maybe not in the same way, but I feel God's effect on my life. I can see the fingerprints He has left on the world: the beauty of nature, the songs and tunes, the gift of thought, and a heart capable of loving. I know of no other way the universe could exist without a God who made it all. You talk of science, but there is no purely scientific explanation for Christian experience, for beauty, for music, for intelligence, for love, and for the very first cause of the universe itself. But these things are real, and the Bible explains what science does not."

What a mouthful, I mused, *and quite truthful; what will the professor say now?*

There was no rebuttal to the student's lengthy answer; rather, a second question was posed: "I suppose you believe in obeying archaic Victorian morality as a part of your Christian beliefs?"

The freshman hesitated before saying, "If you are referring to moral laws like the Ten Commandments, then I do believe in them; but, I am not sure that is the same thing as Victorian morality. I believe we should do our best to obey God's moral laws as we must obey scientific laws. When you break a scientific law you hurt yourself, and when you break a moral law you hurt yourself. Over five thousand years of history show that when societies honor the Ten Commandments they usually prosper, and when they do not they normally decay and fall. This fact is a partial explanation why our own campus is plagued with problems of dishonesty, drugs, alcohol, and venereal disease. If the Ten Commandments were obeyed, would we have these problems?"

The professor challenged the student's historical analysis. He also tried to score some points by thrusting her in a corner with a reference to the German Christian pastor Dietrich Bonhoeffer, who involved himself in the plot to assassinate Adolph Hitler. "Was he justified in ignoring the prohibition against killing?" the professor asked. "If not, are not the commandments too inflexible?"

Just when it seemed the student was going down for the count, she came up swinging: "I am not that familiar with the Bonhoeffer affair, but as a Christian I believe there are basic rules of morality just as there are basic rules of grammar. But when I read the Bible I do not feel that I must wear a straitjacket. What I need is a God-guided conscience that will help me in my real life situation."

After a few moments of lingering debate over morality, the professor turned the topic with another question: "Do you believe in immortality? If so, how can you believe that we who die and decay can live again?"

"I do and I can," came the reply. With a sense of exasperation the professor declared, "This is unbelievable! It simply means you have never faced the finality of death."

A long, tense silence followed. Then, with tears glistening in her eyes, the young girl stunned the class: "Sir, both of my parents were killed in a car accident last year. I watched as their bodies were lowered into the grave. I cried and cried. And then I cried some more. It still hurts deeply when I think about it; but I know that my father and mother were more than a few pieces of mangled flesh and bones. They were human beings. And just as energy cannot be destroyed, life cannot be destroyed. Physically we die, but there is much more to life than that. During this time I experienced something that you may not understand but something that you and nobody else can deny. That something was the 'peace that passes all understanding.' God made all the difference in the world to me then. He does now." That ended the discussion. A telling witness for Christ had been made, even if all the questions were not fully answered.

It may all sound rather incredible. I, too, was amazed by the incident, but that is the way it actually happened. As a timid "silent debater," I was never the same after hearing an unsophisticated but earnest girl for all practical purposes out-debate her professor. True, there were some "holes" in her arguments. A sophisticated, argumentative philosopher could have latched on to them. *But she tried* — and her arguments were not too bad. The point is, every person probably left class that day having a higher opinion of Christianity. No one may have been directly converted as a result of the student's stand, but everyone heard an unashamed Christian challenge the arguments of a good but skeptical thinker. And that in itself may well have given birth to many second thoughts and a new curiosity about the things of God. If that occurred, a successful witness had taken place.

That is what all believers must learn to do — even if one is not philosophical or very able in argumentation. Moreover, it can be done. People can, in love, be helped to reevaluate their position and become more open to the gospel of Jesus Christ. But should we Christians really attempt it at all if people are blasé and skeptical?

WHY WITNESS?

Whether or not we find witnessing comfortable, there is a rapidly increasing and compelling need for believers to have the courage and ability to defend and commend the Christian faith to the doubter. The reason is obvious. We are living in an age of escalating skepticism, humanism, scientism, and materialism where more and more people have difficulty believing in a God they cannot see. Not only that, many doubters and unbelievers feel that the church, although it is a believing community, is not a thinking community. Consequently, the skeptical thinker may assume he has to surrender his mind in order to believe in the God of the Bible. Also, we must honestly face, as Langdon Gilkey pointed out, that even in our churches there are those with serious doubts.[1] All this points to the compelling need to learn how to answer doubting questions. That is why we should learn to witness to the skeptic effectively.

The church needs concerned Christians who possess some expertise in presenting helpful answers to the arguments against their faith. Our responsibility is to offer some sensible reasons for what we believe. The apostle Peter stated it: "Sanctify Christ as Lord in your hearts, always being ready to make a defense to everyone who asks you to give an account

1. Langdon Gilkey, *Naming the Whirlwind* (New York: Bobbs-Merrill, 1969), pp. 181-82.

for the hope that is in you, yet with gentleness and rever-
ence" (1 Peter 3:15). If people choose to ignore or reject
Christ after being confronted with the reasonableness of
Christianity, then it is their responsibility. But they have the
right to hear a coherent presentation of the faith. That puts
the burden on us who believe. Our responsibility is to help
them work through their honest doubts. Until that is carried
out, we are to that extent culpable for their rejection of
Christ. Therefore, we must try to answer whatever doubt or
skepticism that separates them from a saving knowledge of
Jesus Christ. That brings us to the second basic question:
How do we carry out our responsibility?

HOW TO WITNESS

Answering skeptical doubters involves not only knowing
what to say but *how* to say it. Therefore, before examining
several specific skeptical arguments and a suggested Christian answer — which is the bulk of this book — we must
carefully consider how to say it.

In the first place, a Christian must pray for God's guidance,
patience, and understanding; that goes without saying. Anyone who would communicate Christ effectively must do it in
the wisdom and power of the Spirit of Christ — and with love
and concern. Mere argumentation rarely convinces or wins
anyone. That is especially true if a person is closed and his or
her doubts are not truly *honest* doubts. Our argumentation
will rarely touch or move that person. That brand of skeptic
quite often has some sort of moral problem and rather than
face it, he tends to retreat into skepticism. Many, it seems,
reject Christ because they still prefer to remain in sin and
refuse the leadership of Jesus in their lives. If that situation
persists, their doubts and skepticism are hardly honest. That
is another problem to be dealt with forthrightly. But if a person is honest in his doubts, we believers can help. Through
God's guidance and loving patience we can find a way into
the very heart, mind, and soul of the sincere skeptic. In order
to reach him, therefore, we must learn to identify with him in
the dynamic of his problems. That is what love demands.

Moreover, the incarnation, "God with us," is not a mere
theological proposition; it is a practical principle to be understood and applied. As Christ became flesh to reach out and
save us, we must exemplify the same attitude. To impact

others, a willingness to identify with them in the spirit of the incarnation is vital. The challenge for all Christians is to thrust ourselves in the worst of all places — among the poorest of the poor, the sickest of the sick, the loneliest of the lonely, and the most skeptical of the skeptics — just as Jesus did.

Often, we Christians seem to be too interested in protecting ourselves from every form of pain and doubt. Instead, we should find ourselves in the poverty-stricken ghettos, pain-wrenched hospitals, and doubt-ridden circles of the skeptics wherever they are found. Picking up one's cross and following Christ results in experiencing the joys and sorrows, faith and doubts of people whom we seek to reach and touch with God's love. There is no cross without identification and no identification without sacrifice.

To identify with and talk to the skeptic will not be easy to learn, however. Paul Tournier said, "Listen to the conversations of the world. They are for the most part dialogues of the deaf. A person speaks in order to set forth his own ideas, in order to justify himself, in order to enhance himself."[2] Is that what the skeptic sees in the witnessing of high pressure Christians? Hopefully not! We are to be willing to *listen to* and *empathize with* people. Paul Tournier knows that communicating effectively with people requires Christian sensitivity in which one identifies with "the innumerable throng of men and women laden down with their secrets, fears, sufferings, sorrows, disappointments and guilts."[3] To reach the doubter demands that we become genuinely concerned with the flesh and blood skeptic.

In learning how to share with the skeptic, the foundational question we face is why so many reasonable, able, and thinking people — not to mention many less able — have been so dogmatic in their denunciation of belief in God. For example, Thomas Edison declared that "religion is all bunk."[4] Edison's denunciation seems quite unreasonable when he himself admitted how little he knew about the universe. He stated, "We don't know the millionth part of one per cent about anything. We don't know what water is. We don't know what

---

2. Paul Tournier, *To Understand Each Other* (Atlanta: John Knox, 1976), p. 8.
3. Ibid., p. 49.
4. George Seldes, comp., *The Great Quotations* (New York: Pocket Books, 1967), p. 816.

light is. We don't know what gravitation is. We don't know what electricity is. We don't know what heat is. We have a lot of hypotheses about these things, but that is all."[5] Yet he outright denied the Christian faith. Why? The answer to that fundamental question is first found by seeking to understand the heart, mind, and inner soul of such skeptical personalities. Something brought them to their doubts. Some experience — probably negative — gave birth to their skepticism. Therefore, we must try to grasp their subjective philosophy, that is, their inner experiences.

John Warren Steen, in his book *Conquering Inner Space*, cites several possible reasons people become skeptics. He gives examples such as the absence of a child-father relationship, a rebellion against an overly strict home, disillusionment with organized religion, excessive egocentricity, a genuine problem reconciling the reality of evil with a good God, and so on.[6] Once we penetrate the surface of what we may perceive as hard-boiled or blasé skepticism, we will soon see a person who needs to be understood, loved, and respected — not rejected. In a word, we must love him, yet at the same time not be intimidated by his skeptical line.

We Christians do have some helpful answers to doubts. But first we must learn to love the doubter and accept him as a personality created in God's image and for whom Christ died. If we keep that fact before our spiritual eyes, we will discover that we can learn to care for even the most militant anti-Christian; not because he may become a mere trophy to be won in a religious debate, but because we see him without Christ, lost and lonely. The principle is plain: People are reached primarily through love, not insensitive argumentation alone. We learn to "argue" well because we love them and seek to win them to Jesus Christ.

Further, dealing with the doubter demands self-confidence, but that must not be tainted with any form of self-righteousness or intellectual pride. The normal but harmful temptation to preach at and argue against the various forms of skepticism and atheism must be resisted. "Don't preach to me!" is the cry of rebellion when one tries it.

At a civic club luncheon one day, the conversation centered on atheism. One rather sanctimonious saint recited

5. H. S. Vigeveno, *Is It Real?* (Glendale, Calif.: Regal, 1971), p. 6.
6. John Warren Steen, *Conquering Inner Space* (Nashville: Broadman, 1964), pp. 104-6.

Psalm 14:1: "The fool has said in his heart, 'There is no God.'"
"So saith the Word of God," he arrogantly stated, implying
that all atheists are fools. In a sense that is true, but it is
doubtful that our Lord Jesus Christ would quote such a
Scripture when trying to reach an atheist. Jesus preached to
and talked with people, but He never preached down to
anyone or belittled their personhood. He was firm and frank;
He did it all in humility and love.

A few years ago, America's first lady of atheism, Madelyn
Murray O'Hair, and the former "Chaplain of Bourbon Street,"
Bob Harrington, debated Christianity. Thousands heard them.
Unfortunately their conversations were virtually bereft of
any constructive dialogue. Caustic debates between believers
and non-believers always tend to degenerate into fruitless
verbal battles that do little to enhance the image of Christianity — or atheism. We may learn to out-argue a person, but
that does not guarantee success unless we have demonstrated the spirit of Christ's love in what we have said and
done.

Yet at the same time, we must have an answer for the
skeptic. It will not do to be loving but silent. Much good can
come from a positive presentation of our faith that makes
sense to the skeptical mind. That is the primary reason for
this book. Although no attempt is made to be too profound or
verbose, this book is designed to help the average witness
share with doubting people — to present Jesus Christ intelligently and lovingly.

The skeptical arguments may seem formidable, but we
have no reason to fear; our faith is rooted in truth. Our only
problem arises when our ignorance of the available weapons
leaves us defenseless. And in the light of today's world we
cannot afford the liability of being illiterate, powerless Christians. A believer must know the arguments for and against
the faith.

The format of this book is to investigate several significant
personalities who have been influential skeptics. Although
these persons and their thought structures are not delved
into in great depth, each one represents a brand or form of
unbelief that boasts a host of contemporary followers. They
will serve as symbols to aid us in finding some answers to the
arguments of the many skeptics around us. It is hoped that
answers can be put in the hands of those who will lovingly
and intelligently witness for Christ to today's doubters and
unbelievers. Take courage; you can respond to a skeptic.

2

The Psychological Skeptic

Religion is an obsessional neurosis based on illusions, fulfill-
ments of the oldest, strongest and most insistent wishes of
mankind.

— Sigmund Freud, psychoanalyst (1856-1939)

THE PSYCHOLOGICAL ARGUMENT

Sigmund Freud, Viennese psychiatrist, stands as the symbol — if not the father — of the psychological skeptic. He was
born May 6, 1856, in the town of Freiburg, Moravia. Growing
up in Vienna, he became one of the most controversial and
influential makers of modern thought. As Freud began to
explore and chart the unknown world of the subconscious or
unconscious mind, he gave birth to many revolutionary ideas,
expressed in such terms as *id, ego, superego, repression,* and
Oedipus complex. By tracing the cause and cure for many
mental illnesses to subconscious memories, he fathered psychoanalysis. Virtually everyone knows his name and has
acquired at least somewhat of a grasp of his startling ideas.

Freud's new approach to the frightening realm of mental
and emotional illness, along with his preoccupation with the
role of sex in human behavior, cause some to place a serious
question mark over psychoanalysis. More than a few have
seriously disagreed with the Austrian doctor who dealt with
deep, dark desires supposedly locked within sexually-pos-

sessed subconscious minds. Still, his influence is almost incalculable. Moreover, Sigmund Freud was an outspoken promoter of an essentially atheistic, psychological philosophy. He saw the concept of God as merely the "father projection" desires of an inadequate personality.

Although some strongly opposed Freud's views, they never gained enough power to curtail the universal spread of his insights. His concepts, generally speaking, have become an integral part of Western society. That can be seen not only in the fields of psychology and religion but also in surrealistic art and a stream of writings in various fields.

Christians cannot ignore Freud's incredible impact, especially when his ideas strike at faith in God. Although his expertise was certainly not in religion, the fact that he was a renowned student of the mind who spoke out strongly against our faith requires a response from believers. Of course, we may in some degree agree with Freud as a psychoanalyst — he did develop many helpful concepts — but we must disagree with Freud the religious skeptic.

Sigmund Freud possessed a dominant personality. He could be overpowering, even overbearing at times. Yet he was a man of contrasts; on occasion he appeared quite humble. For example, when someone compared him to great thinkers like Kant and Pasteur, he replied, "I have a high opinion of what I have discovered, but not of myself. Great discoverers are not necessarily great men.[1] And though some people believed him to be "a crazy man who saw sex in everything,"[2] he was happily married for fifty-three years, and whenever he was away from his wife he wrote her daily. His personal courage and strength are well illustrated in his willingness to be a revolutionary and his unwillingness to drug himself even when dying of cancer. He wanted to taste every flavor of life's experiences.

When it came to religion, however, Sigmund Freud was an unrelenting secularist who diagnosed religion as nothing but an "obsessional neurosis" or mere "wish fulfillment." Despite his pride in his Jewishness, it seems he had contempt for the faith of his fathers. He argued that people want and therefore create a nice, fatherly God. They desire some rules to

1. Gerhard Masur, *Prophets of Yesterday* (New York: Harper Colophon, 1966), p. 317.
2. John Rowan Wilson, *The Mind* (New York: Time, 1964), p. 101.

live by and finally enjoy "pie in the sky by and by." He spelled out these views in his book *The Future of an Illusion:*

> [Religious dogmas] are illusions, fulfillments of the oldest, strongest and most insistent wishes of mankind; the secret of their strength is the strength of these wishes. We know already that the terrifying effect of infantile helplessness aroused the need for protection . . . which the father relieved, and that the discovery that this helplessness would continue through the whole life made it necessary to cling to the existence of a father — but this time a more powerful one. Thus the benevolent rule of divine providence allays our anxiety in face of life's dangers, the establishment of a moral world order ensures the fulfillment of the demands of justice, . . . and the prolongation of earthly existence by a future life provides in addition the local and temporal setting for these wish-fulfillments.[3]

In summary, Freud became convinced that people created religion to satisfy what they wanted. He knew, of course, religion has its roots deep in universal needs. He did not superficially dismiss religion; he knew countless people were sincerely religious. Yet he was sure they were wrong and self-deceived. Religion was not based on harsh realities; it was no more than wish fulfillment. Freud felt quite right in criticizing the inadequacy of such people to face life in their own strength. Hence, his rejection of faith in God. Much more could be said about Sigmund Freud, but that is the gist of his argument.

We have all met "Freudians" of one type or another. Many people today, it seems, look at Christianity as merely an escape for the weak; those who cannot face life in the raw. Religion is escapism, mere wish fulfillment, they tell us. Some are not quite that crass, but the general Freudian spirit of skepticism infects many. What can we say to such a skeptic? How can we help that self-assured person who believes he has no need for religion, who sees religion as little more than a crutch for crippled personalities? Granted, it is not easy to present a rationale of the Christian faith to the skeptic who is so strong and tough-minded that he senses no need for God and sees those who do as weak, dependent, and unrealistic.

3. Sigmund Freud, *The Future of Illusion* (New York: Liveright, 1953), p. 52.

AN ANSWER

A noted Christian thinker of our day is Elton Trueblood. In his writings he expresses his deep concern over the psychological onslaught on the faith by the Freudian types. Because of his concern, he has developed a very sensible apologetic, that is, a Christian defense, to meet the attack of this type of skepticism. We can learn from it.

Trueblood first begins by observing, "Freud's approach to the subject [of religion] is, *on the surface,* a very plausible one, so plausible, indeed, that the reader may easily be led along by a line of thought which seems reasonable and fair."[4] Trueblood is right; there is definitely a certain plausibility in Freud, and we must not underestimate the power of the skeptical line. However, although we may respect the initial reasonability of the argument, Trueblood's next point is most telling. Here he gets beyond the superficial plausibility of Freud and points out, "There is no good reason to respect the judgment of an alleged music critic who has not listened to music."[5] His point is that many Freudians set themselves up as religious critics without the most basic credentials; they have never seriously researched the Christian faith in depth. They tend to dismiss it summarily without a fair hearing. They are like the music critic who never listens to music. This fundamental weakness is often found in the Freudian skeptical approach.

UNDERESTIMATING THE RELIGIOUS INSTINCT WITHIN PEOPLE

As previously pointed out, Sigmund Freud and many of his present-day disciples say that all religion is nonessential. Mature, strong people have in themselves all they need. Freud would probably say people need each other, but that is still humanism because it dismisses one's need for a transcendent God to meet life's issues. Could it be that his theory is not sensitive enough to the deep-seated and genuine religious "instinct" that resides in the very core of one's personhood? Seeking contact with the Final Reality is a universal trait of humanity. It is most difficult to argue against it or merely set it aside as wish fulfillment. It is too stubborn a

---

4. D. Elton Trueblood, *Philosophy of Religion* (Grand Rapids: Baker, 1977), p. 181.
5. Ibid., p. 185.

fact for that. But Freudians say all that is of importance in life is material and psychological fulfillment. Final or Ultimate Reality does not matter. Therefore, most of humanity is on a quest for nothing. Is Freud right? Is there no more to life than mere material and behavioristic entities? Are so many people self-deceived? Can the universal religious instinct be so summarily dismissed? Are the Freudians too dogmatic in their dismissal of religion?

The temptations of Jesus can give us insight to answer these questions. When being tempted in the wilderness, Jesus responded to Satan, "It is written, 'Man shall not live on bread alone, but on every word that proceeds out of the mouth of God'" (Matthew 4:4). Jesus' quotation from Deuteronomy 8:3 is simple and straightforward; there is more to life than "bread." This is not true for religious mystics alone; Jesus' statement vibrates the deepest chords of everyone's essential being. As humans we instinctively know there is more to life than our mere physical existence. The psalmist knew in his heart that there was more to human life than meets the eye of the materialists:

> As the deer pants for the water brooks,
> So my soul pants for Thee, O God.
> My soul thirsts for God, for the living God;
> When shall I come and appear before God?
> (Psalm 42:1-2)

We all have a natural, almost irrepressible desire to know the "ground of our being," that is, to discover the bottom line concerning where we come from, who we are, where we are going, and above all, *why?* Through the eons of time, countless people and cultures have testified that these questions are *always* there, and they are a persistent reminder that one cannot be satisfied with mere sex and materialism. W. Somerset Maugham, the famous British novelist — and something of a skeptic himself — shared these thoughts as he approached his ninetieth birthday: "When I look back on my life . . . it seems . . . strangely lacking in reality . . . . It may be that my heart, having found rest nowhere, had some deep . . . craving for God."[6]

The concept of and desire to know the Final Reality is

6. James C. Hefley, *A Dictionary of Illustrations* (Grand Rapids: Zondervan, 1976), p. 98.

inescapably and profoundly "just there." The philosophers would call it an *a priori* given. It all grows out of our essential, basic need to apprehend true meaning in life. And when we begin to seek seriously the final meaning of life, right there we meet God, for He is the only ultimate source of meaning and reality. As Francis Schaeffer put it, God is "the God who is there," and He alone gives meaning to life and that is all that can be said. God as the goal of life in depth is simply a "given." To ignore the need of grasping meaning and God's relation to it, or try to explain it away on mere psychological grounds, is not facing reality in its fullest, deepest dimensions. The religious instinct is far too profound for that. It is there and a part of our deepest reality.

Moreover, that line is a good argument, for these kinds of "given experiences" abound around us in many fields of thought. As the great British philosopher H. D. Lewis said, "We seek the best understanding we can have of the way things are, and at some point, to be very carefully considered before we claim to reach it, *we just affirm that we find things to be this way or that.*"[7] The knowledge and quest for meaning, and thus God, is just the way we find things. Nothing more can be said. That fact is most difficult to refute; it surely cannot be summarily rejected as Freudians tend to do.

Of course, the human search for ultimate meaning and that quest's connection to God need to be made clear to the skeptics. They do connect — obviously. It is difficult to demonstrate that connection, but aspects of it will become increasingly clear as we progress through the following chapters. It can be best summarized by saying that the connection between the reality of God and our quest for life's final meaning rests in the fact that God is our Creator.

Some deny God as the responsible Author of Reality. That calls for more time and argumentation, but many grant at least God's hand in bringing the world into being. And even if they do not, we can ask them to assume it and build on it. He is the "ground of all being." The reasoning is simple: I as a *person* seek life's ultimate ground of my being. Surely that "ground" must be *Personal,* for personhood is the highest concept I can conceive. Thus the ground of my being, life's highest concept, because I am personal, must likewise be *Personal.* Anything less than Personal would not be life's

7. H. D. Lewis, *The Elusive Self* (Philadelphia: Westminster, 1982), p. 37.

highest concept. It is the only logical conclusion. God is no more than the "religious " name for the "Personal Ground of Being."

That is what Genesis 1-3 is all about. We are created in God's image, to be like Him. Since we have sinned and have become estranged from our Creator, our Ground of Being, we are on a profound search to discover life's ultimate meaning, and that "meaning" has to be a personal God and restored personal fellowship with Him. That is the very best explanation of the quest.

Have thinking people through the years seen this principle? History tells us they have. Many philosophers and psychologists — men as able as Freud — have grasped the principle. Great thinkers like Rudolph Otto, C. A. Campbell, Anselm, and a host of others contend that the universal religious instinct is far from weakness or unrealistic, as the skeptic charges. Actually, they realize that to seek meaning and God is to face reality "as we find it." They know personality is reality in its final dimension and alone gives life meaning. Of course, this quest and need for a personal God can be interpreted different ways — as Freud obviously did. It does not conclusively "prove" God; nothing does, for that matter. But then again we are back to the original argument, the quest for meaning and God is just *there*.

Therefore, it seems the most logical interpretation of our quest is that this human need is innately placed there by God. We Christians believe that is what happened in God's creation act; thus we long for Him. Again, we conclude the Christian interpretation of the religious instinct is the wisest because it answers the basic question of life in the most plausible manner.

Carl Jung, one of Sigmund Freud's superstar students and successor in fame, grasped something of the idea. Jung departed from the Freudian view as illustrated on one occasion where he engaged a patient in conversation. He diagnosed her problem: "You are suffering from a loss of faith in God and in a future life." She replied, "But, Dr. Jung, do you believe these doctrines are true?" His response, "That is no business of mine. I am a doctor not a priest. I can only tell you that if you recover your faith you will get well. If you don't, you won't!"[8]

8. E. Stanley Jones, *Abundant Living* (New York: Abingdon, 1942), p. 38.

Not only did Carl Jung disagree with his mentor's belief that faith in a life-fulfilling God is a weakness or evasion of reality, Jung went so far as to contend that faith in God is often a cure for many emotional and social problems. He may have been a long way from being a Christian, but he realized that people are groping for a relationship with their Creator. People not only want the "God who is there," they *need* a relationship with Him. Jung described this quest in the title of his book *Modern Man in Search of a Soul.* Howard J. Clinebell records the most quoted passage from this work: "Among all my patients in the second half of life — that is to say, over thirty-five — there has not been one whose problem in the last resort was not that of finding a religious outlook on life."[9]

Another Viennese psychiatrist, Viktor Frankl, was Jewish like Freud, but unlike Freud he did not escape the Nazi Holocaust. Frankl was imprisoned in the infamous Auschwitz concentration camp in south Poland. There he came face to face with the full fury of Hitler's hell. He experienced life reduced to the bare bone. He got down to the "bottom line" of life — to the precious metal of pure existence. In that setting Frankl discovered that Freud's view of the importance of sex was overestimated. Freud's materialistic analysis of life simply did not make sense in the concentration camp. Frankl learned that when he came to grips with the basics, the importance of religion could not be overstated. A person's greatest and most fundamental need is to find meaning in life, he argued. Frankl learned one must find a place and purpose in this vast universe through a relationship with an almighty, creating God.

In his book *Man's Search for Meaning,* Viktor Frankl gives his testimony concerning what happens to those who do not discover more than bread or sex to give meaning to their lives: "Woe to him who saw no more sense in his life, no aim, no purpose."[10] This survivor of Auschwitz discovered first-hand that faith is not the invention of cowards or the weak, but the unfailing resource of the courageous who are able to face the worst possible problems and suffering.

---

9.   Howard J. Clinebell, Jr., *Basic Types of Pastoral Counseling* (Nashville: Abingdon 1966), p. 250.
10. Viktor Frankl, *Man's Search for Meaning* (New York: Washington Square, 1963), p. 121.

What Frankl experienced in Auschwitz he continued to share in his practice as a psychiatrist. He firmly believed we have genuine and legitimate "inherent tendency" to reach out for meaning — to move beyond the mere physical aspects of our nature. He contended that the idea of God and the human hunger for God is present in all people. How can one therefore dismiss it on mere psychological wish-fulfillment grounds? To do so is almost like dismissing one's own self-consciousness. And that is tragic.

Augustine (354-430) stated long ago what Frankl found to be true during the Holocaust. Augustine said that God has created us for Himself, and our hearts cannot rest until we find rest in Him.

In his "confession," Leo Tolstoy explains his need for God, his compulsion to find a meaning to his existence. This inner drive pushed him beyond suicide. He describes his inherent tendency: "During that whole year, when I was asking myself almost every moment whether I should not end matters with a noose or a bullet . . . my heart was oppressed with a painful feeling, which I can only describe as a search for God. . . . It was a feeling of fear, orphanage, isolation in a strange land, and hope of help from someone."[11] After pursuing this instinct, Tolstoy found what he was looking for. He explained, "I live, really live, only when I feel Him and seek Him. . . . And more than ever before, all within me and around me lit up, and the light did not again abandon me. And I was saved from suicide."[12]

To summarize, Sigmund Freud and his contemporary humanists have grossly underestimated the essential religious instinct and craving within people. There is vastly more to religion than an "obsessional neurosis" or a "wish fulfillment." The Freudians do not have an answer for the patent facts of human existence and the quest for meaning. Faith in God faces it all. Sheldon Vanauken in *A Severe Mercy* describes this fact as he quotes C. S. Lewis:

> A wish may lead to false beliefs, granted. But what does the existence of the wish suggest? At one time I was much impressed by Arnold's line, "Nor does being hungry prove that we have bread." But surely, tho' it doesn't prove that one par-

11. Leo Tolstoy, *A Confession, The Gospel in Brief and What I Believe*, trans. Aylmer Maude (London: Oxford U., 1967), p. 62.
12. Ibid., p. 65.

ticular man will get food, it does prove, that there is such a
thing as food! i.e. if we were a species that didn't normally eat,
weren't designed to eat, would we feel hungry?[13]

That is the point. The quest for meaning points to God.

Ironically, Freud's rejection of the validity of the human
desire for a heavenly Father is strange. The quest is rooted in
his own Jewish tradition. If he had only studied this revelation more carefully he may have seen that what he termed a
"wish fulfillment" is a clear and unmistakable basic "need
fulfillment" arising out of the fact we are creatures fashioned
by a Creator-Father. Again, let it be granted that what has
been put forward in response to Freud, that people sense a
need of God, can be viewed as evidence in favor of Freud's
view — *if God does not exist.* But the most coherent view of
reality is that He does. The quest is too deep and profound to
be rejected as mere superficiality. Thus Freud's view, in the
final analysis, falls to the ground, or at best is very weak and
tenuous. The religious instinct is far too strong a reality.

That brings us to the second psychological error in the philosophy of the skeptical Freudian.

Misunderstanding What the Christian Religion Offers People

Those who embrace the Freudian approach often make
statements like, "Religion is the opiate of the people"; "religion is for old men and women"; "they are in it for the
money"; and so on. Their indictments grow out of the belief
that religion is a comfortable crutch. We as Christians, however, see it as a rugged cross.

One wonders if Freud ever took the time to study objectively and seriously the crux of Christianity — the cross of
Christ. It seems the error of many of his modern disciples, at
any rate. If they would consider the cross, they would realize
that the crux of Christianity contradicts the Freudian idea of
religion. For example, in Matthew 26:36-39 we read,

> Then Jesus came with them to a place called Gethsemane, and
> said to His disciples, "Sit here while I go over there and pray."

13. Sheldon Vanauken, "A Severe Mercy," *Christianity Today* (13 January
    1978), p. 7.

> And He took with Him Peter and the two sons of Zebedee, and began to be grieved and distressed. Then He said to them, "My soul is deeply grieved, to the point of death; remain here and keep watch with Me." And He went a little beyond them, and fell on His face, and prayed, saying, "My Father, if it is possible, let this cup pass from Me; yet not as I will, but as Thou wilt."

Obviously, Jesus did not want to die on the cross. Did His "religion" therefore provide an escape? No! He was *compelled* by His relationship to God to meet head-on the fiercest of evil and to endure the very worst in order to achieve the best. Religion was certainly not a comfortable experience for Jesus. And that principle is the heart of every true follower of Jesus Christ. Genuine Christians do not run from the "crosses," the realities of life. Mature believers are willing to endure them in order to conquer them. The cross is at the heart of it all. We bear our cross as Jesus did. Jesus said,

> Do not think that I came to bring peace on the earth; I did not come to bring peace, but a sword. For I came to set a man against his father, and a daughter against her mother, and a daughter-in-law against her mother-in-law; and a man's enemies will be the members of his household. He who loves father or mother more than Me is not worthy of Me; and he who loves son or daughter more than Me is not worthy of Me. And he who does not take his cross and follow after Me is not worthy of Me. He who has found his life shall lose it, and he who has lost his life for My sake shall find it. (Matthew 10:34-39)

Jesus' words illustrate how Sigmund Freud misunderstood the very basis of Christianity. Christianity never offers us what we selfishly or superficially want in our weakness. There is a cross to be borne. But therein is the divine paradox; in the bearing of our cross we find *the essence of life's fulfillment.* Our Lord emphasized over and again that one finds life as he loses it (Matthew 10:39). The essence of genuine life is found only in Christ and His cross.

The Old Testament is full of that idea also. Jonah did not want to do God's will and preach to the people of Nineveh; but Jonah's religious experience compelled him to do the undesirable. In that he found true life. In all probability, Abram had little desire to leave the peace and prosperity he enjoyed in Ur of the Chaldees. But his religious experience of God demanded his journey into a far-off land. There he became a great man. That certainly is not weakness. Moses obviously had no wish to return to Egypt and lead his people out of slavery; yet his encounter with the living God caused him to realize that he must overcome his reluctance and go. The result? He led his people to freedom, where they found life at its best.

Contrary to what many like Freud suppose, Christianity does not offer what we superficially desire so that life can be more comfortable. More often than not, the cross is in direct opposition to our personal wishes and comfort. Paul was appalled at the thought of believing in Jesus, but his experience on the Damascus road transformed him from a persecutor of Christians into a preacher of Christ and willing martyr. It takes tough people to follow Christ. But in Christ true purpose is found. Life is life in the full when life is lost in self-sacrifice to God's will. The cross is a far cry from a crutch.

Freud further charged Christians as not having the courage to face their honest problems concerning their faith. He declared that believers sweep their doubts under the carpet and are afraid to be honest skeptics. Freud theorized that the men of faith in the Bible were forced to suppress such questions because of socio-religious pressure. Granted, Freud did recognize that most believers have their season of doubt. But again it is obvious that Freud and his followers failed to take the time to study objectively that true Bible believers do *not* suppress their doubts and perplexities, but are willing to express them openly and fully. Moreover, Freud did not see that periodic doubts do not dispel lasting faith.

That skeptical attack fails because of what the Bible says about Moses, Job, Jeremiah, Thomas, and many other scriptural and historical characters who openly confessed their lack of faith and yet believed. The Word of God constantly encourages people to be open and aboveboard with their doubt. In some sense, Jesus Himself exemplified the principle. On the cross our Lord cried, "My God, My God, why hast Thou forsaken Me?" (Matthew 27:46). This cry of utter anguish is a quotation from Psalm 22 where David became overwhelmed with doubts and feelings of isolation. Doubts are never hidden in the Bible. Further, any survey of Christian history indicates that the great men and women of faith were often quick to share their perplexities. They were not afraid to be honest with themselves, others, and God. Why? Because they believed that their faith was based on God's ultimate truth; truth that is not fearful of questions.

So Freudian skeptics often fail to take the time to investigate honestly and objectively the fact that genuine believers do not take the easy road through life. They do not realize that mature and dedicated Christians take the hard path that leads up into the mountains, through the valleys, across the deserts, and into the swamps before reaching the Promised Land. People like Ruth, David, the prophets, the disciples, and the apostle Paul chose a rough, rugged path because of their faith. Their faith was not a crutch.

True Christianity is an invitation to suffering, doubts, trials, and toil. It was and always will be. Yet, right there life takes on reality. Thus the Freudians misunderstand Christianity on two basic points. First, they fail to see that our faith is anything but an escape mechanism. Second, they miss the point that in choosing the cross, the religious instinct is satisfied and meaningful life is discovered. Granted, not all Freudian skeptics make such mistakes, but many do. What a tragedy to miss it all!

Now it must be acknowledged that Freud may have had something legitimate to say about superficial, nominal Christians. His arguments there may be, to some extent, true. But that shallow brand of faith is not what we are arguing for or witnessing about. We desire to help the doubter see the validity and strengths of a true biblical faith. If only Sigmund Freud could have seen that the men and women of faith are the only ones who dared face reality. Albert Einstein, the great Jewish scientist, saw it and paid tribute to the one courageous segment of German society that took a costly stand against Hitler. Einstein described it as the "Confessing Church," a faithful remnant inspired by faith to do what needed to be done no matter what the price. Perhaps the tragedy of Freud was that all he saw was nominal Christianity. We must demonstrate and witness to the real thing.

CONCLUSION

The fundamental rule of disciplined debate is to take an honest look at whatever one is seeking to criticize or refute. Freud seemingly disregarded this when it came to religion. He failed to investigate on a biblical basis his own Jewish faith. It is sad to realize that although he had a brilliant, curious mind, he never studied the greatest book ever written and never knew the greatest Person who ever lived: a fellow Jew and the Savior, Jesus Christ. He never understood true Christianity and so made his skeptical pronouncements.

Many of the doubters we meet today commit, to some degree at least, the same basic blunder. Consequently, they are superficial in their religious concepts. If they would examine the biblical faith sincerely and in depth, they would learn Christians are not weak, wishful people, nor do they retreat from life's realities. True believers simply *have not* missed a meaningful life. They have found it in the cross of Jesus Christ.

Therefore, our task in witnessing to the skeptic is to communicate what faith in God is all about, how it brings meaning to life and thereby dispels the myths. The religious instinct is valid and can be fulfilled. Of course, that means we believers must know and live out that faith in our daily lives. We must never be guilty of Freud's criticisms. We must genuinely face life straight on in Christ's power.

Sigmund Freud died as World War II was breaking out. He died convinced that believing in God was weakness. Our prayer should be that the skeptics we meet will, by our help, recognize the weaknesses in such skepticism and be led to examine the power of genuine Christianity, which does not necessarily offer what we want but what we so basically need.

3

The Suffering Skeptic

Since . . . thc world is shaped by death, mightn't it be better
for God if we refuse to believe in Him, and struggle . . .
against death, without raising our eyes toward heaven where
He sits in silence?
— Albert Camus, existentialist writer (1913-1960)

THE ARGUMENT FROM PAIN AND SUFFERING

Albert Camus was a man of many experiences: soccer
player, actor, playwright, editor, member of the French
underground, community dropout, and novelist. He is well
known as one of the popularizers of what writers and philosophers call existentialism. This approach to life is extremely
difficult to define, for it gathers together thinkers as diver-
gent as Kierkegaard the Christian and Heidegger the atheist.
But in a general way it can be said that existentialists hold to
the idea that meaning and reality are found primarily in one's
personal experiences. Existence is the reality that matters
most. Subjectivity is the base line of reality. Objective truth
and reality is at best secondary. What we experience in our
subjective existence becomes the best judge of value, meaning, truth, and reality. Subjective satisfaction is "where it is,"
say the existentialists.

Although these brief definitions are gross generalizations,
they get at the heart of the movement. Thus a subjective reli-

gious person, such as Kierkegaard, and subjective atheists, such as Albert Camus, Jean-Paul Sartre, and Heidegger, can, in a broad sense, all be termed existentialists.

Albert Camus was well suited to the role of the existentialist; he explored his own human existence in multiple and varied situations. Although he sought to understand his personal existence without reference to God, Camus was not a cold, calculating, antisocial atheist. He, like many skeptics, was a committed humanitarian. And it was this humanitarian existentialism that brought him to skepticism.

Everyone realizes life is often filled with suffering and pain. Camus was deeply moved by the human plight. He knew it firsthand; his life was filled with pain. His father was killed the year he was born. His mother worked as a charwoman in order to support her two sons. Camus himself was tormented by ill health — suffering repeated bouts of tuberculosis. The evils of poverty, disease, and finally Nazism repulsed him. This personal, existential exposure to suffering molded his whole outlook on life. Many of his writings illustrate not only his marvelous literary talent but his identification with and compassion for sufferers. Camus's writings capture the pain and anguish of an existence amidst the scourge of disease and the horrors that life flings at us. He was a man acquainted with grief; thus he developed a profound humanitarian spirit.

Camus's philosophical problem revolved around the fact that he could not bring himself to believe in a good, wise, and powerful God in light of all the suffering in the world. The problem of evil and suffering constantly troubled his mind. His existential experience, which was of central importance in his thought structures, was filled with suffering. No doubt he asked the question a thousand times, "How could a good, powerful God allow such suffering? If God is behind all existence, why all the existential evil?" The quandary was pungently pointed out one day when Camus was asked by a six-year-old girl returning home from church, "Why are little girls in Africa starving while I have plenty to eat? Doesn't God love them as much as he does me?"[1] Camus had no answers; he concluded there was no God.

To a greater or lesser degree, that is the problem of mil-

---

1. S. Paul Schilling, *God in an Age of Atheism* (Nashville: Abingdon, 1969), p. 125.

lions, believers as well as doubters. For example, Rabbi Richard L. Rubenstein identified with Camus's inability to believe in an all-powerful, good God when he struggled to survive the terrifying presence of pain in a Nazi concentration camp. In his book *After Auschwitz*, Rubenstein stated that the death of 6 million Jews spelled the death of his faith in the God of Abraham, Isaac, and Jacob.

This quandary is perhaps the most serious and widespread type of skepticism we face in witnessing for Christ. However, before the problem of pain can be properly addressed, we must have a clear grasp of the issue. We will consider the problem of pain through the writings of Albert Camus.

The Plague stands as one of Camus's most moving novels. In its pages the existentialist expresses his acute awareness of the human dilemma. One writer said, "The plague . . . causing untold suffering and death to thousands of innocent children as well as hardened sinners, represents the universal condition of mankind."[2] Dr. Rieux, Camus's main character in the novel, is presented as the compassionate non-Christian physician who is fighting the scourge. In a conversation with Jean Tarrou, another fascinating character in the book, Dr. Rieux speaks with intensity: "Since the order of the world is shaped by death, mightn't it be better for God if we refuse to believe in Him, or struggle with all our might against death, without raising our eyes toward heaven where He sits in silence?"[3]

These last five words — "where He sits in silence" — vibrate with Camus's anger and frustration at God. *The Plague* clearly reveals Camus's assumption that "cruelty comes from God while compassion is *our* virtue."[4] Turning again to the conversation between Tarrou and Dr. Rieux, Tarrou asks where Dr. Rieux learned his "de-Christianized humanitarianism." The doctor replies promptly with one piercing word: "Suffering."[5] In an existential response to suffering, Camus severed his relations with a supposedly silent God while he resolved to fight a lonely and seemingly absurd battle against "The Plague."

2. C. Stephen Evans, *Despair: A Moment or a Way of Life?* (Downer's Grove, Ill.: InterVarsity, 1971), p. 30.
3. Albert Camus, *The Plague*, trans. Stuart Gilbert (Harmondsworth, England: Penguin, 1968), pp. 107-8.
4. George Buttrick, *God, Pain and Evil* (Nashville: Abingdon, 1966), p. 150.
5. Camus, p. 108.

In a sense, Camus represents the finest of non-believing existentialists and has expressed an extremely difficult argument. We Christians are constantly confronted with it as we try to witness. No doubt you have raised the issue yourself.

Archibald MacLeish expresses the dilemma in its harshest terms: "If God is God He is not good; if God is good He is not God."[6] That is a terrible dilemma. Perhaps it is overstated; yet, the problem is real. This timeless problem was formulated in its more classical style by Epicurus (341-270 B.C.). Epicurus argued that once we recognize the reality and evil of suffering (as Camus and millions of others have) we are forced to choose one of four options if we believe in a God of goodness.

1. God wills to remove evil but cannot.
2. God can and will not.
3. God cannot and will not.
4. God wills to remove evil and can.[7]

Epicurus stated the issue better than MacLeish, and it does give one some options. Now it is clear that only the fourth choice is open to biblical Christians. This option, however, immediately presents two basic questions. First, does God love those in pain? And, second, if He does, why does He not send immediate relief? Camus and his kin concluded that God did not love; therefore, they cannot love God. Camus felt it is less painful to reject belief in a loving God. Believers take the opposite view. Yet, Elton Trueblood has seen the seriousness of the issue clearly when he says, "So far as rational faith is concerned the problem of evil is our most serious contemporary difficulty."[8]

That is not a new challenge, of course. Contemporary existentialists did not invent the problem. Long ago Job confronted the inescapable reality of suffering and, above all, the treacherous anxiety it causes. The psalm writer faced the same fundamental problem: "Why dost Thou stand afar off, O Lord? Why dost Thou hide Thyself in times of trouble?" (Psalm 10:1).

6. S. Paul Schilling, *God and Human Anguish* (Nashville: Abingdon, 1977), p. 46.
7. John Hick, *Evil and the God of Love* (Glasgow, Scotland: Collins, 1977), p. 5.
8. D. Elton Trueblood, *Philosophy of Religion* (Grand Rapids: Baker, 1973), p. 231.

While chained in the galleys of a slave ship, John Knox, the great Scottish preacher and reformer, experienced inner "anger, wrath, and indignation . . . conceived against God, calling His promises in doubt."[9] So did Increase Mather, the Puritan theologian, who while suffering wrote that he "was grievously molested with temptations to atheism."[10] The Bible and Bible believers, however, have not failed to face up to the issue. As contemporary Christians, it is encouraging to realize that we have centuries of biblical thought, often refined through suffering, to draw upon as we attempt to respond to the existentialist skeptic and help him in his doubts.

In 1697 the German philosopher Leibnitz wrote a book entitled *Theodicee*. This word, coined by Leibnitz, means "an effort to vindicate the justice and righteousness of God in ordering or permitting evil and suffering in His creation."[11] The technical term for the study has since then been called *theodicy*. And Leibnitz's work is just one of many such efforts. Throughout history Christians have been well aware of the problem of pain and have posed many helpful answers. We believers have discovered we do have a "theodicee," or answer, and it must become part and parcel of our faith in Christ if we are to witness to the doubter. As Christians who cling to the old rugged cross, stained with suffering and shame, we know there is an answer that is at the very heart of Christianity. If we can grasp that answer, it will not only help the skeptical existentialist, we will also help multitudes of troubled believers, not to mention our own struggles.

A CAUTION

Before attempting an answer to the dilemma of suffering, we must be careful to avoid a temptation that tends to afflict us all, namely, superficiality in replying to a most difficult question. If we have no answer, we must be honest about it. It never pays to pawn off a superficial answer to a knotty problem. Honesty is vital to an effective witness.

As a young pastor, I encountered this full force while leading a church-sponsored retreat for college students. While sitting on a mountain cabin porch chatting with the students,

9. Harry Emerson Fosdick, *Dear Mr. Brown* (New York: Harper and Row, 1961), p. 67.
10. Ibid., p. 67.
11. Schilling, *God and Human Anguish*, p. 55.

I expected to face some tough if not unanswerable questions. However, this time all went surprisingly well, at least so I thought. The young people were very generous in the questions they asked and even more gracious in the answers they accepted (or at least tolerated without undue argument). They even seemed to accept my rather inadequate answer to the last and most troublesome question: Why does God allow so many people to suffer in so many ways? As we adjourned I was relatively pleased with my replies. I thoroughly enjoyed being complimented by our minister of youth who said, "Great job, Pastor."

My self-satisfaction was shattered, however, when Janis, one of our adult counselors, asked to have a word with me in private. As we talked she unburdened her frustration: my last answer missed her by a wide mark. She said, "I have been in the church all my life. I was taught to sing about God's love. I really do believe in God and His love. But I also know there is excessive pain in this world, and it seems so much of it is unnecessary and plain unmerciful and unfair! How do I really begin to understand why a good God causes or at least allows all the evil of suffering?"

Here was a mature Christian, a well-educated woman in her mid-forties, who was shaken by the problem of pain. No glib answer would satisfy Janis. This experience dramatically pointed out that we must come up with some real content to solve the issue. Doubters demand it. Superficiality will not suffice.

A BIBLICAL AND CONTEMPORARY APPROACH TOWARDS AN ANSWER TO SUFFERING

We will begin to solve the question by referring to one of the oldest books in the Bible. The book of Job tells the story of a remarkably good man. God allowed Satan to rob Job of his possessions, his children, and his health. He lost everything, absolutely everything, except life itself — and that seemed to hang by a thread.

The book of Job presents the problem of suffering at its worst. We see the acme of disasters befalling the best of people. As Philip Yancey observed, "No one deserved suffering less than Job; no one suffered more."[12] Job is a glaring and

12. Philip Yancey, "When Bad Things Happen to Good People," *Christianity Today* (5 August 1983), p. 23.

challenging case that compels attention.

In Job we have a fourfold view of suffering. The Bible story illustrates every kind of pain. Job suffered *emotionally* when he lost his children and possesssions. Job suffered *physically* when his body broke out with painful sores. Job suffered *mentally* when he could not understand why he was suffering so much. Finally, and worst of all, Job suffered *spiritually* when he was tempted to curse the Creator and commit suicide: "Then his wife said to him, 'Do you still hold fast your integrity? Curse God and die!'" (Job 2:9). That is suffering! He stands out as a sufferer striving to understand his pain.

Moreover, the book of Job pictures him as someone with whom we can identify. As David M. Howard expressed it, "The reader may interact with Job as a man who struggled with the problems very similar to the ones with which modern man is struggling."[13] Although he was a righteous man, he was no idealized superman. He had the same weaknesses we do. That is exemplified in the following passages that exhibit self-pity, anger, and pure misery:

> I know that Thou wilt not acquit me.
> I am accounted wicked,
> Why then should I toil in vain?
>
> (Job 9:28-29)

> But I would speak to the Almighty,
> And I desire to argue with God.
>
> (Job 13:3)

> When I expected good, then evil came,
> When I waited for light, then darkness came.
> I am seething within, and cannot relax;
> Days of affliction confront me.
> I go about mourning without comfort;
> I stand up in the assembly and cry out for help.
> I have become a brother of jackals,
> And a companion of ostriches.
> My skin turns black on me,
> And my bones burn with fever.

13. David M. Howard, *How Come, God?* (New York: A. J. Holman, 1972), p. 12.

Therefore my harp is turned to mourning,
And my flute to the sound of those who weep.
                                    (Job 30:26-31)

We can understand Job's feelings. He is one of us: a mere human being created by a great God. But he learned to triumph over suffering. That is remarkable. What did Job learn?

Two common misunderstandings about suffering are corrected in Job's experience. First, Job's friends were wrong in blaming him for his suffering. Just because he was a great sufferer did not mean he was a great sinner. Sin brings suffering, but not *all* suffering is the result of one's personal sin. For example, my sin was not the cause of a tornado that swept through our city a few years ago and took several lives and caused millions of dollars of damage. Job did not suffer because he was a great sinner. In fact God condemned that accusation that came from Job's friends: "The Lord said to Eliphaz the Temanite, 'My wrath is kindled against you and against your two friends, because you have not spoken of Me what is right'" (Job 42:7).

At times, of course, we are clearly the cause of our suffering. When we suffer for our own sin, it is not a theological problem. But often the righteous person will suffer more while the sinful person will suffer less. That phenomenon is found in the Bible and continues today. Although judgment of sin is a partial answer to suffering, it is not the total solution, and it precipitates misunderstanding when applied too generally.

A second misunderstanding centers on Job's wife. She was wrong in blaming God for Job's suffering and in urging her husband to curse God and die. Many people mistakenly think that sickness, natural disaster (so-called "acts of God"), economic catastrophes, and so on are the design of God. That is a gross misrepresentation. We are told that Satan, *not God,* caused Job's suffering. God does *not* bring about evil. He despises it. Therefore, we are not to blame Him. Satan is the author of evil.

Yet, at the same time, we are compelled to admit a loving God does *permit* suffering. That constitutes the mystery. We would like to know why, but there are aspects of God's permissive will that are inscrutable. There are things God allows that cannot be understood. Why God grants Satan a seemingly free hand is one of those mysteries. Our task is to rest on the *love* and *goodness* of God, though we do not fully understand it. All of life is filled with mysteries. This is one of them. Because life is this way we must learn to rest in it. And although God permits suffering, we cannot rightly blame Him for it, even if it comes to us a mystery. (This aspect of the problem will be taken up again shortly.)

Leslie Weatherhead addresses the error of blaming God in his powerful book *The Will of God.* He cites the case of a good friend who was grieving over the loss of his wife. His friend said, "Well, I must just accept it. It is the will of God."[14]

Weatherhead disagreed. He pointed out that the husband was himself a doctor and for weeks had been fighting for his wife's life. He had called in the best specialists in London. He had used all the devices of modern science. Was he all that time fighting against the will of God, Weatherhead asked? If she had recovered, would he not have called her recovery the will of God? Yet we cannot have it both ways, the preacher argued.[15]

In a word, we must help the doubter realize God is *not* the author of evil, even if we cannot always understand why He permits pain. That fact is well confirmed in the life of Jesus, who lovingly revealed God's desire to comfort and cure the sick.

The book of Job thus begins to deal with the problem of suffering by providing us with a fellow sufferer with whom we can identify. It prohibits us from blaming God or Job for his suffering. That is a good beginning; it answers two very important questions. Job then goes on to further resolve the agonizing question.

Real help is found in Job's personal encounter with God as recorded in chapter 38, verses 1-4:

> Then the Lord answered Job out of the whirlwind and said,
> Who is this that darkens counsel
> By words without knowledge?
> Now gird up your loins like a man,
> And I will ask you, and you instruct Me!
> Where were you when I laid the foundation of the earth!
> Tell Me, if you have understanding.

14. Leslie D. Weatherhead, *The Will of God* (Nashville: Abingdon, 1977), p. 9.
15. Ibid.

God wanted Job to know he could not fully understand
suffering.

Remember, we look through a glass dimly. C. S. Lewis, a
contemporary writer on the issue of suffering, learned how
humbling that fact was for Job and also for us. After losing
his wife to cancer and struggling through the grief process, C.
S. Lewis saw that "the problem of pain" (the title of his masterful book) is not removed by human logic, even the best
logic. In a sense, God cannot explain all we desire to know
because He is infinite and we are finite. Lewis wrote in his
classic *A Grief Observed*, "When I lay these questions before
God I get no answer, but a rather special sort of 'no answer.'
It is not the locked door. It is more like a silent, certainly not
uncompassionate, gaze. As though He shook His head not in
refusal but waiving the question. Like, 'Peace, Child; you
don't understand'"[16]

That may sound like sidestepping the issue, but that is not
so. It puts us in our place as limited human beings. We simply
cannot grasp all of God's actions. To recognize and accept
that fact is an important step, a humbling one. But we will
only find help as we humble ourselves before God.

Furthermore, although we may in our pride believe that
we and our world are fundamentally good, there is the harsh
reality of the Fall. Genesis 3 declares dramatically that we
are a fallen people living in a fallen world. In *Man: The Image
of God*, G. C. Berkouwer writes, "Our attention is directed to
what man has done with and in his humanity, in his fall away
from God, which affected tremendously every nook and
cranny of his being and existence."[17]

Philip Yancey, in his book *Where Is God When It Hurts?*,
calls our world "The Stained Planet." This world, he says, is
"a good thing, bent."[18] He believes that the "existence of suffering on this earth is . . . a scream to all of us that something
is wrong . . . that the entire human condition is out of
whack."[19] As seen in the Fall, sin inevitably brings suffering.

G. K. Chesterton, another contemporary, gives an eloquent
sketch of life on a planet scarred and disfigured by sin and

16. C. S. Lewis, *A Grief Observed* (London: Faber and Faber, 1961), pp. 54-55.
17. G. C. Berkouwer, *Man: The Image of God* (Grand Rapids: Eerdmans,
    1969), p. 120.
18. Philip Yancey, *Where Is God When It Hurts?* (Grand Rapids: Zondervan,
    1978), p. 51.
19. Ibid., p. 56.

pain. He observed, "According to Christianity, in making it [the world], He set it free. God had written, not so much a poem, but rather a play; a play he had planned as perfect, but which had necessarily been left to human actors and stage-managers, who had since made a great mess of it."[20]

When we think of how we human beings can rise to grandeur and then sink to squalor, we cannot help but say, "Yes, Chesterton is right, something is radically wrong." And when we focus on what happened to the most loving and innocent Person who has ever lived, Jesus Christ, then the cross reminds us that life is terribly flawed, undoubtedly bent and twisted from what it was meant to be. In a world like this, suffering to some degree is absolutely unavoidable. We must just face and accept that fact.

Then why did God allow the Fall to occur in the first place? The Bible answers that central question. In Genesis, a vital principle stands out: God created us with a free choice. We can choose good or evil. Both goodness and evil are rooted in free choice, and freedom of choice is one of the precious gifts God has given. Freedom alone makes good truly good and, of course, evil truly evil. God did not make us robots. That gracious gift of freedom is the best design, even if evil does result. No real fellowship with God could be possible without it. God cannot have communion with a machine but only with persons who can freely choose Him or reject Him. Thus we make real choices, and that opens up the possibility for evil as well as good. Tragically, we have often misused our freedom and made the wrong choice — not just in the beginning, but throughout history.

Being created in God's image, we have freedom — the power to help or hurt, build up or tear down, go forward or backward. Freedom is always an expensive commodity. For example, a free, democratic society has many social problems that a controlled, autocratic society eliminates. That is why sociological revolutionaries like B. F. Skinner want to erase freedom as we know it in order to create a society without crime, pollution, poverty, and other such problems. But we would lose more than we could possibly gain. And if God had created us with no freedom, unable to choose sin and its inevitable consequences, we would lose *far* more than we would ever gain. To pose the proposition that God could

20. G. K. Chesterton, *Orthodoxy* (Garden City, N. J.: Doubleday, 1959), p. 78.

create us with freedom and yet make it impossible for us to sin is an absurdity, and God is not absurd.

Therefore, because of the whole complex subject of freedom, which in many respects is beyond us, God may not see fit to remove the burden of suffering in our temporal world. But one glorious day He will. Moreover, He strengthens the heart, mind, soul, and body of sufferers who seek to endure and conquer pain. When we experience God's presence, inspiring and empowering us in our struggle, then we begin to reach that point where we say we can trust God, even if we cannot always understand His ways. Job voiced his pain-refined testimony in Job 42:2-6:

> I know that Thou canst do all things,
> And that no purpose of Thine can be thwarted.
> "Who is this that hides counsel without knowledge?"
> Therefore I have declared that which I did not understand,
> Things too wonderful for me, which I did not know.
> "Hear now, and I will speak;
> I will ask Thee, and do Thou instruct me."
> I have heard of Thee by the hearing of the ear;
> But now my eyes see Thee;
> Therefore I retract,
> And I repent in dust and ashes.

God does help us and come to our aid when in true humility, "in dust and ashes," we look to Him, see Him, and trust ourselves to Him. And there is another principle about pain.

Vernon Bittner's book *Make Your Illness Count* teaches us to see our suffering selves not just as victims but as students — students growing into maturity. Alexander Solzhenitsyn suffered terribly both in prison and in a cancer ward while in Russia. Solzhenitsyn made an almost mind-boggling comment about his experience: "Bless you prison, bless you."[21] Why did he say that? Because in prison he came to see that the object of life is not ease but the maturity of the human soul. That lesson enabled him to turn the tables on pain, for his suffering deepened and matured him as a person.

In April 1819, John Keats wrote to his sister and brother saying that "hardships, anxieties, troubles, and annoyances" in life should be seen as a "vale of Soul-making," out of

---

21. "Why Charles Colson's Heart Is Still in Prison," *Christianity Today* (16 September 1983), p. 13.

which can emerge "personal identity — genuine individuality."[22] Simply put, suffering can bring good out of bad. Even though we live in a stained world, as John Hick points out, it is a "place in which true human goodness can occur and in which loving sympathy and compassionate self-sacrifice can take place."[23] When that happens victims become victors. God has not deserted us.

Not only that, one day Christians will be victorious over all evil and suffering. The time will come when Jesus Christ returns and *all* wrong will be put right. There will be an end to it all. Therefore, the apostle Paul said, "I consider that the sufferings of this present time are not worth comparing with the glory that is to be revealed in us" (Romans 8:18). That is comforting.

Albert Camus failed to understand the Christian view of God and suffering because he assumed God deserted the human race. He came to believe that our suffering is like Sisyphus in his parable story *The Myth of Sisyphus.* Sisyphus was doomed to push a big rock up a mountain, but the rock would always come tumbling down. But Sisyphus did nothing but keep trying. That does not make sense. And Camus believed that life itself does not make sense.

However, he missed something in his narrative. In the Sisyphus story Camus admits that if we are not alone in our suffering, if somehow the universe knows how to love and suffer, then we could find meaning and peace (reconciliation).[24] But that is the point of the entire Christ event; *we are not alone in our suffering*. As Christians, we believe in an ever-present God who loves us. All we have said up to this point demonstrates that comforting reality. Therefore, even in the depths of human anguish we can find meaning and peace that passes all understanding. Furthermore, God is not only with us, He also suffers with us. The message of Christianity, the good news, is that God not only loves us and hears our cries for help, He comes to us as a fellow sufferer. That is a marvelous answer to the problem of pain.

Dr. Joseph Boutwell of the Center for Disease Control in Atlanta reminds us there is a limit to suffering. Pain and suffering do not go on forever. What a relief that is. That is an

22. Schilling, *God and Human Anguish,* p. 146.
23. Hick, pp. 371-72.
24. Schilling, *God and Human Anguish,* p. 257.

eternal truth as well as a *temporal* reality. There is full redemption in Jesus Christ, who comes to suffer with us and die for us — thus redeeming us from evil and its resulting pain. God comes to us to save us from every effect of the Fall. All creation will one day be put right. There is a judgment coming. God will do the right thing.

Remember the apostle Paul said, "The creation waits eagerly for the revealing of the sons of God. For the creation was subjected to futility, not of its own will, but because of Him who subjected it, in hope that the creation itself also will be set free from its slavery to corruption into the freedom of the glory of the children of God" (Romans 8:19-21). In the midst of it all, God shows Himself as a fellow sufferer and eternal Redeemer.

As Christians, we believe that by turning to Christ and surrendering our lives to Him we can by faith begin to face, endure, and conquer the worst of problems. True, we do not have all the answers or a completely satisfying solution to this complex and puzzling quandary, but we do have marvelous helps, and *faith can take one the rest of the way*. Faith is the victory that overcomes the world (1 John 5:4). In this context, George Buttrick shares a personal experience: "Not soon shall I forget the words of a parishioner as he died from the scourge [cancer]. He was as realistic a man as I have known. His churchgoing was not the kind which clamors for 'religious emotion.' Yet his last words were almost rapture: 'If you could see the Plan.'"[25] Even in the dark valley of death the man of faith could see "the Plan." God had become the light of his life. There are realities to this life where faith alone is the final answer.

Obviously, there is much that can be said in response to Camus's unwillingness to believe in a good, all-powerful God while living in a world shattered by suffering. A Christian can face the ugly fact of evil and pain, no matter how problematic such a reality may be.

CONCLUSION

At the beginning of this chapter we quoted Richard Rubenstein, the Jewish rabbi who said that, after Auschwitz, Jews can no longer believe in a good and all-powerful God. Al-

---

25. Buttrick, p. 51.

though she was not a Jew, Corrie ten Boom suffered through the hell of a concentration camp. Yet she did not lose her faith. She discovered that God was alive and near — a God who enabled her to endure the unendurable and conquer the unconquerable. Corrie ten Boom, like many of us, expressed doubts and frustration. She cried out like Jesus on the cross, "My God, My God, why hast Thou forsaken Me?" But by faith she came to know that God had not forsaken her; He was there identifying with her pain. She learned that the words of the apostle Paul are true:

> And we know that God causes all things to work together for good to those who love God, to those who are called according to His purpose. . . . Who shall separate us from the love of Christ? Shall tribulation, or distress, or persecution, or famine, or nakedness, or peril, or sword? Just as it is written, "For Thy sake we are being put to death all day long; We were considered as sheep to be slaughtered." But in all these things we overwhelmingly conquer through Him who loved us. For I am convinced that neither death, nor life, nor angels, nor principalities, nor things present, nor things to come, nor powers, nor height, nor depth, nor any other created thing, shall be able to separate us from the love of God, which is in Christ Jesus our Lord. (Romans 8:28, 35-39)

Let us share this glorious message with the suffering doubter.

4
The Scientific Skeptic

Modern science makes it impossible to believe in a personal
God.

—Aldous Huxley, author (1894-1963)

THE HUXLEYS AND THEIR ARGUMENTS

Thomas Huxley, grandfather of well-known Aldous Huxley, achieved notoriety as a scientific skeptic. Born near London, trained as a surgeon, he became a famous figure in the
field of zoology, who accepted, defended, and propounded
Darwin's theory of evolution. Historians have described him
as "Darwin's bulldog" and "Darwin's general agent." Being
more than a pure scientific evolutionist, Huxley also became,
to use his own word, an agnostic. Because of his philosophy
of science, he was convinced that, in principle, we cannot
know whether there is a God or not. As a scientific evolutionist and religious agnostic (not that one *necessarily* implies the
other), Huxley stands as a forceful spokesman for those who
believe that religion is anti-scientific and needs to be exposed
and eradicated as an antiquated and unrealistic world view.

Unfortunately for Christians, Thomas Huxley scored a brilliant victory — at least as many saw it — in a debate over
evolution with the well-known bishop of Oxford, Samuel
Wilberforce. Huxley succeeded in portraying the bishop as
eloquent, but ignorant and prejudiced against scientific inves-

tigation. In a flair of sarcasm, Wilberforce asked Huxley
whether a person should trace his ancestry back to the apes
through his grandfather or grandmother — not a very wise
question to pose to an astute, brilliant scientist. Huxley's
reply devastated the bishop. He said he would prefer to be
the descendant of a humble monkey than of a prejudiced
man.[1]

Huxley no doubt proved to be an able critic of Christianity.
Although he labeled himself an agnostic, he actually preached
a "practical" atheism. And he preached it well. Huxley convinced many that religion was unfriendly, unnecessary, and
above all, unscientific. He came to that position when he discovered how *unfriendly* many religious people were because
of his defense of Darwin. He concluded that religion feared
science and, therefore, stood as an enemy of science. Huxley
also felt religion was *unnecessary*. While Charles Darwin
never denied the need for a Supreme Being, Huxley did. He
held that nature was its own creator. He believed everything
happened by mere chance. Further, this scientist-preacher of
agnosticism proclaimed that religion was *unscientific* because
there was no way to "prove" on scientific grounds the reality
of God.

Thomas Huxley's grandsons, Julian and Aldous, followed in
their grandfather's footsteps. Sir Julian Huxley, a notable
botanist, received a knighthood for his scientific accom-
plishments. He also became an influential humanist and the
first director-general of the United Nations Education, Scientific, and Cultural Organization (UNESCO). As a teacher and
writer, Sir Julian Huxley lobbied for scientific humanism to
replace Christianity and all other "supernatural religions."

Sir Julian's brother, Aldous, is best known as the author of
the classic twentieth-century novel of a "soul-less, stream-
lined Eden" entitled *Brave New World*. Although not a scientist, Aldous Huxley wrote, "Modern science makes it impossible to believe in a personal God."[2] He found his "reality" in
drugs rather than Christianity. As an existentialist drug experi-
menter, he set out to savor the ultimate experience through
narcotics. In his controversial book *The Doors to Perception*,

---

1. Alec Vidler, *The Church in an Age of Revolution* (Baltimore: Penguin
    Books, 1968), p. 117.
2. Rheinallt Natlais Williams, *Faith, Facts, History, Science and How They
    Fit Together* (Wheaton, Ill.: Tyndale, 1973), p. 59.

Huxley advocated the use of drugs for everyone. Tragically, he practiced what he preached until his death.

Thinkers and writers such as Thomas, Julian, and Aldous Huxley, men of great achievement, often influence people to assume automatically, uncritically, and blindly the idea that transcendental religion and science are incompatible. Of course, such a view is not held by all people of science. Sir Francis Bacon, a scientist of tremendous stature, referred to the Bible as the Book of God's Word and nature as the Book of God's Works. Bacon believed that not only a disciplined study of the Bible points to God, but a disciplined study of nature likewise reveals God. Sir Isaac Newton held similar views, as did the mathematician Blaise Pascal. Therefore, it hardly seems wise to reject religion automatically on scientific grounds.

The contemporary problem for the witnessing Christian is that the scientific skeptic's viewpoint is widespread and often goes unchallenged by today's secular society. Many have followed their lead without an investigation of the subject. And that attitude continues to grow.

Anyone who has attempted to share his faith, especially to university students, has encountered this Huxlian brand of skepticism. For example, schools in England are required to provide a time for Bible reading to integrate religion with social studies, mathematics, science, and other subjects. But one day, after a science teacher finished reading the required Scripture passage for the day, he closed the Bible and said, "And now let us turn to something real."[3] As Sir Richard Gregory put it:

> My grandfather preached the gospel of Christ.
> My father preached the gospel of socialism.
> I preach the gospel of science.[4]

That approach has permeated the Western world. The following excerpt from an anonymous letter to the editor published in a recent *Atlanta Journal* indicates how militant antireligious feelings can actually be, even in the heart of America's so-called "Bible Belt." The writer, attacking belief in creationism, stated:

3. Ibid., p. 57.
4. Michael Green, *Faith for the Non-Religious* (Wheaton: Tyndale, 1976), p. 37.

What is distressing is that such absurd beliefs persist as we near the 21st century. It may be viewed, however, if looked at objectively, as a twitch in the death throes of an outdated and nearly defunct theology. . . . It is unfortunate, but man has always tended to mysticize everything he does not understand. Until the susceptibility is weeded out through further evolutionary advance this medieval idiocy will hang around our necks like an albatross. But be sure, the day will come when the doors of the last church will close forever. The last Bible will be shipped off to some museum where it will gather dust along with the implements of other medicine men and shamans who, for a time, controlled men's minds. Some future archeologists may look through this silly book and be amused that his ancestors were so gullible.

Even if relatively few are so crass in their views, this mentality is everywhere. These are issues we must face. How is the Christian to reply? Is there an answer to this dogmatic, non-critical rejection of our faith?

AN ANSWER

The basic question becomes, Is there really an irreconcilable conflict between modern science and our "ancient" faith, as the Huxleys declared? The Christian obviously answers *no*. And that is not dogmatism, because this negative response is supported by a careful and critical examination of science's "mother," laws, dangers, and limits. If the agnostic will face these issues, he may have second thoughts concerning his off-the-cuff rejection of the faith.

Of course it is only fair to grant that some agnostics with the scientific mind-set are true investigators of religious faith and because of their scientific presuppositions still reject Christianity. That is a different matter. To argue on a presuppositional basis is a quite technical philosophical pursuit and thus beyond the scope of this book. Still, *many* scientific thinkers have refused the faith non-critically. To those of this uncritical attitude, we should present what will follow. Help for the more critical type will be presented later.

THE MOTHER OF SCIENCE

When the Huxleys and other scientific skeptics contend that religion is the enemy of science, they often refer to such incidents as the Medieval church prohibiting Galileo from teaching the scientific fact that the earth revolves on its axis and moves in orbit around the sun. We must confess that on occasion an ignorant church suppressed realities revealed by science. There are cases where the church has been absolutely wrong. And that is still a problem. We have already noted Bishop Wilberforce's blunder. We should not hide it; it never helps the unbeliever when we refuse to face our own mistakes. However, these human weaknesses within the church do not mean that Christianity *in principle* is against science. What is surprising, if not shocking, to those who accept and advocate the Huxlian view is that Christianity is actually the "Mother of Modern Science."

Alfred North Whitehead, one of the world's foremost philosophers, stated in a lecture at Harvard University that Christianity is rightly called the "Mother of Science." He contended that Christianity gave birth to modern science by teaching people to believe in a God who created an orderly, law-abiding universe that could be studied, understood, and managed by people who had been created with investigative, logical minds. Newton, Bacon, Pascal, and many contemporaries have all grasped the concept. This no doubt explains why Christianized Europe became the birthplace of modern science rather than Asia or Africa.

The religions of those cultures tend to teach that nature is imaginary and unreal, often evil. Because of Christianity, Europe came to understand that nature is real and tangible and good. While many religious world views teach that nature is full of gods or is merely an extension of God Himself and therefore taboo and off-limits to curious minds, Christians are taught to believe that God fashioned nature and wants people to subdue and rule it (Genesis 1:28). For the Christian, nature is essentially good and full of potential—after all, God made it.

Moreover, the Bible makes it clear that nature moves in the context of the understandable laws of God, thus opening it up to scientific investigation. Therefore, it is not surprising that while some cultures and religions stagnated science, Europe and Christianity gave birth to the scientific, industrial, and technological revolutions. And it is important to realize, as pointed out, more than a few of the early scientists were earnest believing Christians themselves.

THE LAWS OF SCIENCE

Do the established laws of science really support the skeptical views of the Huxleys? No, at least not in any final sense. Consider the following illustration.

A Christian visited the Soviet Union. He and his Russian guide became involved in a conversation about religion and science. The guide said, "Does anyone with a scientific education believe in God nowadays?" The Christian replied, "Yes, I was not aware of any scientific arguments against belief in God." The guide said in astonishment, "Are you serious?" The Christian replied, "Certainly! Would you agree that during the past seventy-odd years scientists have discovered hundreds of thousands of facts?" After receiving an affirmative response the Christian continued, "Could you name one such fact so discovered that contradicts the idea of God?"[5]

Good question! There are no scientific laws that incontestably refute belief in God. Of course, no scientific law can prove God's existence either. But none rule it out. Furthermore, there is a positive aspect of the issue; there are scientific laws that at least point to the reality of God.

There is what might be called the *law of laws*. This has already been hinted at. The fact that science is grounded on law and order means that science believes that nature, in its essence, is not merely a whimsical, nonsensical mass of atoms acting in caprice. Law prevails everywhere, or scientific laws would not be laws at all and hence undiscoverable. Without the general principle of order, science simply would not be. Now law and order could not just happen. Randomness is much more likely to beget randomness. Cause and effect prevail throughout our very complex universe. Therefore, it is most reasonable that there should be a first, orderly cause—and that is what believers call God. Law and order implies a Lawgiver of law and order. Therefore, in the final analysis, science points to an intelligent Creator.

Further, agnostics often say if scientists ever learn to create life that would disprove God. That is hardly true. The same argument holds: When life is created using our ordered minds to arrange matter in a proper manner to produce life, that is a reminder of the fact that it takes an ordered intelligence to create life in the first place. Again, order does not just happen.

Thus to hold that the universe exists by God's hand dem-

5. J. Edwin Orr, *The Faith That Persuades* (New York: Harper and Row, 1977), p. 3.

onstrates more logic than to say that the concept of God is mere superstition and natural laws just happened. God has created in His own ordered way, and our own orderly creativity points to Him.

That argument has traditionally been called the cosmological proof for God. That is, the universe is a cosmos, not a chaos. Thus it had to have an intelligent, orderly Creator. And though the argument does not *prove* God, it certainly points in that direction and makes more sense than uncritical skepticism.

C. S. Lewis in his book *Miracles* argues from rationality. He describes a fundamental rule of reasoning: "No thought is valid if it can be fully explained as the result of irrational causes."[6] Once we accept that basic rule, it is difficult to hold to the skeptical idea that everything occurred by mere, irrational chance. It really isn't rational, Lewis would say. Lewis quotes J. B. S. Haldane here: "If my mental processes are determined wholly by the motions of atoms in my brain, I have no reason to suppose that my beliefs are true . . . and hence I have no reason for supposing my brain to be composed of atoms."[7]

There has to be law and order to allow for the rational thinking upon which the scientist depends to formulate his concepts. That somewhat combines Lewis's argument for rationality with the cosmological argument, but it is legitimate to do so, as cosmology and rationality are certainly not incompatible and imply each other. If, as the Huxleys and scientific skeptics declare, everything that exists came about by mere chance, neither we nor they could even think rationally because we would be in violation of the law of logic: Irrational causes cannot produce a rational conclusion. And science is built on rational thought using empirical investigation.

As a result, the scientific, skeptical argument against God has, in some sense, undercut the very foundation stone of true science. If Huxley is right, rational science is on very shaky ground. The fact is, the basic law of logic supports the Christian belief in "rational, ordered happenings." Science and religion should join hands, not separate.

There is more evidence for God in this general approach,

6. C. S. Lewis, *Miracles* (London: Geoffrey Bles, 1959), p. 27.
7. Ibid., p. 29.

such as the so-called teleological proof for God. This argument points out that all things in the universe move to an end
and purpose. Therefore, there must be a final end, and God is
the "End." Likewise, there is help in the law of entropy.

The law of entropy, known also as the second law of ther-
modynamics, places science itself on the witness stand and
virtually forces it to testify in behalf of belief in some kind of
Supreme Being or Intelligence. A scientific study of the law
of entropy reveals that the universe not only could not create
itself but could not keep itself going without some Supernatural Force from beyond itself. Sir Arthur Eddington described
this law as the greatest law of physics.

Perhaps the clearest and most concise definition of the law
of entropy is found in the picture of a clock that is running
down. W. R. Inge states the argument, "If the universe is
running down like a clock, the clock must have been wound
up at a date which we could name if we knew it. The world,
if it is to have an end in time, must have had a beginning in
time."[8] As best we can discern from science, our universe is
not a self-winding clock but rather one that had to be wound
up at some point: "In the beginning. . ." (Genesis 1:1). The
further scientists probe into the essence of reality, the more
they realize there was a beginning. They even date it some 15
to 30 billion years ago. The universe is finite; all agree to that.
Therefore the universe is dependent upon some sort of beginning outside itself.

Astrophysicists thus talk about the "Big Bang" of creation.
Even if the "Big Bang" was the inevitable explosion of a
gigantic black hole, and even if the universe continues to
expand or comes back in on itself eventually, where did the
first black hole come from? One eventually has to face that
question. And to say it always existed is to give it an ultimate,
eternal quality, which makes it God. And we learned earlier
that ultimacy must be "personal"; thus we are back where we
started — with God. There seemingly has to be some sort of
personal first cause for our finite universe.

Granted, there are some extreme cynics who argue there is
no "first" state. Yet that is difficult to imagine and is extremely
cynical in light of the fact that our universe is limited and
finite. And what about the law of entropy that most all scien-

8.   D. Elton Trueblood, *Philosophy of Religion* (Grand Rapids: Baker, 1977),
     p. 104.

tists agree to? Some further say that Christians beg the question in assuming a first cause and arguing from there. Well, we do assume a first cause. But one has to begin somewhere, and it appears far more logical to assume it than to deny it, even if we appear to beg the question. We must make some sort of leap somewhere to even begin. We all have our presuppositions, including the scientist. The question is: Is the Christian presupposition better than the cynical presupposition? On pure objective grounds, it appears it is.

In principle, that is what Genesis 1 is all about. It tells us what—or more correctly who—the First Cause was. Although all this does not prove God, and involves presuppositions, true science does not in any way conflict with Scripture. They support one another. The supposed science-religion conflict grows out of ignorance of the basic principles of science, the Bible, or both.

A fourth argument can be called the law of open-mindedness. The Huxleys were quick to condemn the closed-minded rigidity of such churchmen as Bishop Wilberforce. And justifiably so! All thoughtful advance—religious and scientific—has grown up because of a healthy, constructive open-mindedness that inspires investigation and creativity. However, the law of open-mindedness conflicts with the Huxleys' dogmatic dismissal of miracles, a transcendent God, and so on. They thus appear to be as closed-minded and dogmatic as some narrow-minded religionists. Both are wrong.

Furthermore, the argument that scientific laws leave no room for miracles is weak. After all, science is built on observation, and what if observation demonstrates a miracle? There is ample reliable testimony to observable miracles. That has been true through eons of time. C. S. Lewis helps us see the error in scientific dogmatism when he compares their interpretation of natural laws to a beginner or critic in the field of poetry: "One often finds that the beginner, who has just mastered the strict formal rules, is over-punctilious and pedantic about them. And the mere critic . . . may be more pedantic still. The classical writers were shocked at the 'irregularity' or 'licenses' of Shakespeare."[9]

Dogmatic narrow-mindedness in science may leave no room for miracles, but if it does, it also leaves no room for the true scientific spirit of open-endedness. Thus it contra-

9. Lewis, p. 116.

dicts its own methodology. Lewis states that the best illustration of this bias against miracles is found in Bergson's reference to a painting. Lewis presents it and criticizes it as follows:

> Let us suppose a race of people whose peculiar mental limitation compels them to regard a painting as something made up of little coloured dots which have been put together like a mosaic. Studying the brushwork of a great painting through their magnifying glasses, they discover more and more complicated relations between the dots, and sort these relations out, with great toil, into certain regularities. Their labour will not be in vain. These regularities will in fact "work"; they will cover most of the facts. But if they go on to conclude that any departure from them would be unworthy of the painter, and an arbitrary breaking of his own rules, they will be far astray. For the regularities they have observed never were the rule the painter was following. What they painfully reconstruct from a million dots, arranged in an agonizing complexity, he really produced with a single lightning-quick turn of the wrist, his eye meanwhile taking in the canvass as a whole and his mind obeying laws of composition which the observers, counting their dots, have not yet come within sight of, and perhaps never will. I do not say that the normalities of Nature are unreal. The living fountain of divine energy, solidified for purposes of this spatio-temporal Nature into bodies moving in space and time, and thence, by our abstract thought, turned into mathematical formula, does in fact, for us, commonly fall into such and such patterns. In finding out those patterns we are therefore gaining real, and often useful, knowledge. But to think that a disturbance of them would constitute a breach of the living rule and organic unity whereby God, from His own point of view, works, is a mistake. If miracles do occur then we may be sure that not to have wrought them would be the real inconsistency.[10]

Sharing that with the doubter and encouraging him to give an open-minded, fair hearing to the realities of God bursting in all around us is a wise course.

THE DANGERS OF SCIENCE

It is odd that Aldous Huxley said that "modern science makes it impossible to believe in a personal God." In the light of his writings we could well have expected him to say: "It is

10. Ibid., pp. 117-18.

impossible for man to survive as a free person without religion." His classic book, *Brave New World,* depicts what happens when religion is buried and science is worshiped as god. *Brave New World* is a horror story about a hell on earth. It chronicles what occurs where there is science without religion, which Huxley saw as a society without meaning—perhaps even without morality. Granted, morality can exist in atheism, but it is doubtful it would survive or have real profundity or high motivation. Why, it can be asked, did Huxley hold such views on God that seem in a sense to violate his own quest for a "brave new world"?

But more frightening than Huxley's fictional account of what may happen tomorrow are the factual accounts of what is actually occurring today as a result of the rejection of God's controlling presence. Those who recommend drastic changes in morality, economy, liberty, and even our own personal identity because of their throwing off the "restraints" of God, never do society a service. If one thinks it an exaggeration to list the dangers of science without religion, reflect upon what has happened in the twentieth century. (Chapter ten presents a more detailed discussion of this issue.)

THE LIMITS OF SCIENCE

The fact is, a pure scientific approach is too narrow and limited a base on which to build an entire world view. The reason is, it cannot unravel the greatest mystery of all: *Why* does everything exist? True, science can tell us much about the what, when, how, and where of things. That comprises science's task—and science has done a credible job. But what about the essential *why* of reality? We are grateful for all science has done and how it has enhanced life and understanding. We believers do not disparage that at all. Christians are not an enemy of true science. We are its friend. But it simply does not give us all the answers. Actually, science is not designed to do so. Its epistemology, that is, its understanding of the source of truth, precludes an answer to the question: Why do things exist? And that is the most vital issue. But science cannot even attempt an answer. Its own presuppositions and methodology do not allow it. Yet *God* can give an answer to that central query. Therefore, it is quite narrow for the scientist to say that his system of truth (epistemology) is the *only* one, and thus dismiss the concept of God.

Of course, not all scientists take this line. The great Sir Isaac Newton was a well-balanced, open thinker. He wanted to know *how* the universe worked as a good scientist, but he also desired to understand *why* it existed. He saw the study of science dealing with the *how,* while the study of Christianity dealt with the *why.* He did not restrict his inquiry to just scientific truth. He was open to all reality.

J. Edwin Orr presents an excellent illustration on this point:

> Does science explain anything? Come into my kitchen and ask me, "Why is the kettle boiling?" I reply, "The kettle is boiling because the combustion of the gas transfers heat to the bottom of the kettle which, being a good conductor, transfers it immediately to the water. The molecules of water become agitated; they spin around and make a singing noise, and finally give off water in the form of steam; and that is why the kettle is boiling." Then my wife comes into the kitchen, and you ask her, "Why is the kettle boiling?" And she tells you: "The kettle is boiling because I am going to make you some tea." I did not tell you why the kettle was boiling. I told you how the kettle was boiling. And science does not tell us the why of anything, really, but only the how and what.[11]

Scientist Robert Jastrow goes even further in a comment about the beginning of the universe:

> Now we see how the astronomical evidence leads to a biblical view of the origin of the world . . . . This is an exceedingly strange development, unexpected by all but the theologians. They have always believed the word of the Bible. But we scientists did not expect to find evidence for an abrupt beginning because we have had until recently such extraordinary success in tracing the chain of cause and effect backward in time . . . . At this moment it seems as though science will never be able to raise the curtain on the mystery of creation. For the scientist who has lived by faith in the power of reason, the story ends like a bad dream. He has scaled the mountains of ignorance; he is about to conquer the highest peak; as he pulls himself over the final rock, he is greeted by a band of the theologians who have been sitting there for centuries.[12]

Science can only go so far. Many open scientists acknowledge that. Thinkers should not lock themselves into any nar-

---

11. Orr, *The Earth That Persuades,* p. 8.
12. Clark H. Pinnock, *Reason Enough: A Case for the Christian Faith* (Downers Grove, Ill.: InterVarsity, 1980), pp. 62-63.

row system of truth, scientific or biblical. All should be open to all reality. Moreover, it is also most significant that science's own trail tends to point to God.

There is one more profound limitation of the skeptic's scientific stance: its inability to explain its own impotence in the face of death. Even the magic of medical technology can delay death only so long. Marvelous indeed is the fact that science has prolonged significantly the expected life span. But we still die. What then? Somehow we all innately sense there is more to life than our few short years on earth. Eternity is bred in us all, even though some may deny it. The following personal testimony, given by a scientist, pretty well says it all:

> My father and mother were deeply religious. My brother and I had no time for religion. We thought that religion was all right for old people, but we were scientists and we thought we had found our way through what we were pleased to call scientific methods. Then my brother was killed. My father and mother had resources, and with their resources they could meet that shattering loss. But I had no one. I had no resources at all.[13]

After his world collapsed, the scientist conducted a personal experiment that demonstrated to his satisfaction that God truly does exist. He accepted Jesus' invitation to turn to Him, and he was not disappointed.

CONCLUSION

We believe that genuine science and biblical religion do not contradict one another but in fact complement each other. In the final analysis, they are not to be divided in two camps at all. All truth is of God, and thus there is a basic unity of all reality: scientific, social, psychological, religious, and so on. Science makes its contribution as does religion. That is important to realize. Let us make peace; truth is at stake. We must all be humble in the face of a complex reality. Together we can explore all that reality is and find truth where it is to be found.

13. Robert J. Dean, *How Can We Believe?* (Nashville: Broadman, 1978), p. 25.

5

The Self-Sufficient Skeptic

God is dead.
—Friedrich Nietzsche, philosopher (1844-1900)

THE SKEPTICAL PHILOSOPHER AND HIS ARGUMENT

Friedrich Nietzsche boasted of himself as a skeptical philosopher of the first magnitude. Through the last one hundred years, multitudes have been influenced and conditioned by his humanistic thought, even if they do not accept the more radical aspects of his ideas. Why does he attract so many? The answer is quite simple. He was a visionary advocate of becoming a self-sufficient, strong-willed superman. And he saw that as the necessary antidote to being a "meek Christian." He was determined to achieve aggressive self-sufficiency through *The Will to Power*. That humanistic approach always has its appeal.

Nietzsche's rebellious attitude was, at least partially, the result of growing up in a home dominated by Christian femininity. Born in Prussia on October 15, 1844, he has been described as "the child of Darwin and the brother of Bismarck."[1] Like many of his age, he became intrigued and inspired by what Darwin theorized as "the survival of the fittest," as well as by Bismarck's rule as an "iron chancellor."

1. Will Durant, *The Story of Philosophy* (New York: Pocket Library, 1958), p. 401.

Although Nietzsche was nicknamed "the little minister" by his childhood friends, by the age of eighteen he determined to cut the apron strings that tied him to God and anyone or anything that might interfere with his quest for ultimate self-acquired, humanistic independence.

His whole life and philosophy emerged out of an agonizing attempt to attain independence and freedom, to become his own god and see his prediction come true, namely, that the future would divide itself into "Before Nietzsche" and "After Nietzsche."[2] A rather presumptuous if not arrogant thought! He authored a form of humanism gone berserk.

Friedrich Nietzsche's restless rebelliousness, expressed dramatically in his writings, shows he had the mind of a brilliant philosopher, the heart of a perceptive poet, and the soul of a self-willed atheist. Nietzsche's unusual and provocative genius produced a life filled with contrasts: He was the atheistic son in a family of devout Christian ministers; his intelligence failed to be recognized until he was insane and almost dead; after his death he became known as a precursor of the Nazis, but, conversely, he stood as a fierce opponent of anti-Semitism. His life can be characterized as both heroic and tragic. He was a heroic man who fought courageously and often violently to overcome illness (migraine headaches, stomach trouble, insomnia, and bad eyesight, prior to insanity) and loneliness (the loss of his father, friends, and a potential wife). Yet in his struggles he only succeeded in losing his health, friends, and his greatest desire: utter self-independence.

Nietzsche's philosophical travels led him to an insane asylum before he was rescued by his mother who took care of him until she died. Then his sister nursed him. The promoter of the concept of a self-made superman, or *overman*, came full circle. He had struggled long and hard through his own personal power to break away from the beliefs, values, and what he termed the "meekness" of his home life, only to end up powerless and under the care of his Christian mother and sister. The philosophical prodigal son was brought home by those who loved him and displayed a quiet, compassionate strength, emanating from their faith in God. His own family, though it had its weaknesses (they were apparently prejudiced against the Jews), became the strong guardians of the

2. Ibid., p. 445.

man who had equated Christian meekness with repugnant weakness.

During his prime, Nietzsche contemptuously condemned the faith of his family. He was convinced that growing up and becoming a real self meant cutting away from parental rules and regulations. A part of this for Nietzsche involved severing the religious ties of the past that bound him to biblical laws and principles. He strove to be a man of faith—not in God, but totally in his human self. He used three words to picture what he saw as the greatest event of history, three words that have become his most famous, or infamous, statement: "God is dead."[3] He no longer needed God; he was free. Human self-sufficiency was attained. God was gone — dead.

Although scores of our contemporaries may not be quite as cavalier as Nietzsche, a basic self-sufficient attitude is everywhere in the humanistic self-effort to "do your own thing," God not withstanding. Granted, all humanists are certainly not atheists; yet, self-sufficiency precipitates a practical atheism that God may as well be dead as far as pragmatic matters are concerned. (The theology of the death of God is more fully discussed in chapter eight.)

Nietzsche the radical argued that "the man of faith, the believer, is *necessarily* a small type of man."[4] In his opinion, such a person is bound to a "slave morality" (Christian ethics) that stifles human freedom and self-development. Thus, he urged his readers to become supermen, to become people who were willing to grow up enough to surrender any religious ideas that would prevent them from making their own laws, doing their own thing, and achieving self-sufficient power. That is how to be an authentic person.

In Nietzsche's classic book *Thus Spoke Zarathustra*, which he rather proudly saw as second to none, he said that Jesus died too young, stating that if Jesus had lived longer He would have revoked His teaching. How sad is Nietzsche's misunderstanding of Jesus; perhaps sadder still his misunderstanding of his own life and teaching. How tragic is the life of the skeptic who tries to live life *alone* as Nietzsche did. What is our answer to the one who rejects the gospel on humanistic, self-sufficiency grounds?

3. Friedrich Nietzsche, *The Will to Power*, ed. and trans. Walter Kaufman and R. J. Hollingdale (New York: Random, 1967), p. 506.
4. Ibid., p. 45.

AN ANSWER

Although we may have little sympathy for Nietzsche the anti-Christian philosopher, we cannot help but feel a sense of sorrow for Nietzsche the suffering man. He lived a tragic life, promoting a tragic philosophy that brings no final joy or peace. Yet, his ideas — at least in embryonic form — are obviously popular today. How do we approach this type of skepticism?

To begin with, realize that Nietzsche's approach is neither new nor novel, let alone true. It is as old as the book of Genesis. His position is almost a carbon copy of Genesis 3:1-8.

> Now the serpent was more crafty than any beast of the field which the Lord God had made. And he said to the woman, "Indeed, has God said, 'You shall not eat from any tree of the garden'?"
>
> And the woman said to the serpent, "From the fruit of the trees of the garden we may eat; but from the fruit of the tree which is in the middle of the garden, God has said, 'You shall not eat from it or touch it, lest you die.'"
>
> And the serpent said to the woman, "You surely shall not die! For God knows that in the day you eat from it your eyes will be opened, and you will be like God, knowing good and evil."
>
> When the woman saw that the tree was good for food, and that it was a delight to the eyes, and that the tree was desirable to make one wise, she took from its fruit and ate; and she gave also to her husband with her, and he ate.
>
> Then the eyes of both of them were opened, and they knew that they were naked; and they sewed fig leaves together and made themselves loin coverings.
>
> And they heard the sound of the Lord God walking in the garden in the cool of the day, and the man and his wife hid themselves from the presence of the Lord among the trees of the garden.

Nietzsche would have said that the Genesis story is as mythological as the story of Achilles. But any serious student of human nature has to admit that the biblical account presents insightful truth. It possesses the ring of reality. What does this Genesis story say to the skeptic of Nietzsche's kind?

The first truth found in Eden is that evil often comes camouflaged in a most subtle way. The serpent is a crafty, conniving con artist. He begins his conversation by carefully planting seeds of doubt: "Has God really said. . . ?" Some of the most vicious characters in history have demonstrated great skill in being able to disguise evil with attractive deception, manipulating people with slick half-truths while playing on people's destructive emotions. For example, a crafty twentieth-century admirer of Friedrich Nietzsche wrote the following words in his book *Mein Kampf:* "Through clever and constant application of propaganda, people can be made to see paradise as hell, and also the other way round, to consider the most wretched sort of life as paradise."[5]

Why do people seem so susceptible to deception? The fact is, we are more readily deceived than we would like to admit. To go it alone and try to become as God, as did Adam and Eve, is unbelievably attractive. We love to be self-sufficient, to play God; but the end result is self-deception. We believers, in attempting to share the truth of Christ with the humanistic skeptic, should point out that people love the self-deception that they can become as God. Sleek half-truths are often worse than an outright lie. It is very easy for each of us to fall into that trap all over again.

The second truth in Genesis, already implied, is the simple, observable fact that whatever is forbidden always seems most attractive. The grass looks greener on the other side of the fence. We all have a rather perverted tendency to focus our desires on what we do not have rather than on what we do possess.

That truth is described by Jesus in His parable of the prodigal son (Luke 15:11-24). The young man in the story grew dissatisfied with the abundance he had. Like Nietzsche, he felt he had come of age; he had to do his own thing. After all, he was self-sufficient. So the prodigal moved out to break the bonds of restrictions; off he went to conquer the world, only to end up in a pigpen—not as a free man but as an enslaved animal. A life of self-independence from God always ends up in some sort of pigpen. An honest, objective look at life shows self-sufficiency to be a lie.

Nietzsche, sounding like the ancient serpent, would have us believe that faith in God is restrictive and protective, forbidding freedom. True, some religious systems are like that, but genuine Christianity is not. When we come to grips with the real message of the Bible, we soon discover that our Father is neither overly restrictive nor protective.

5. George Seldes, comp., *The Great Quotations* (New York: Pocket Books, 1967), p. 786.

From the very beginning, God granted mankind the privilege of ruling creation. We are to "rule the world," even as Nietzsche in a rather bizarre way advocated. But if we are going to govern our world as mature, authentic beings, we must learn to govern ourselves. And that is only possible through faith in God. The self-discipline of faith is the only key to growing up, to coming of age. We simply cannot do it on our own. No one can. To think we can is not self-sufficiency; it is self-deception. It takes "God with us" to accomplish true, free selfhood. God gave us laws of life, designed to keep us from hurting ourselves. When the Israelites ignored God and His commandments, when they did their own thing, they deteriorated into weakness and divisions. As a result, they were conquered and enslaved. Christ and His way alone leads to genuine freedom. That is why the message of Christ is called *good news*. That message enables us to grow into true selves.

At the same time, God is not overly protective as Nietzsche and many contemporaries imagine. God is loving and merciful, but He does not baby us. Like a wise parent, He allows us to come to grips with life, even if it means getting knocked down. He expects us to fight the fight of faith, make decisions in the light of His will, and accept full responsibility for our thoughts and actions. He will be there to provide guidance, comfort, help, strength, and forgiveness when we need it, which is all the time, for we are dependent creatures and not supermen. "In Him we live and move and exist" (Acts 17:28). Yet that utter dependence is such that it does not destroy freedom and responsibility. The point is, one does not have to reject God to be free and responsible.

It is fascinating to observe that skeptics like Nietzsche accuse the Judeo-Christian God of hedging us in, while others, like Rabbi Rubenstein for example, condemn God for not having put a protective shield around the Jews to insulate them from the holocaust. On one hand God is depicted as being too strict, on the other too permissive. In actual fact, He neither babies nor neglects us. There is a middle ground that might be termed a razor's edge, which only God and those who follow Him can walk. One thing is certain — God is never so restrictive that He eliminates human freedom and responsibility. Neitzsche's argument simply falls short.

Nietzsche echoes the serpent again when he contends that we only find true freedom in breaking away from God. We all long for freedom and rightly so. But can inner freedom be found outside of Jesus Christ? The facts do not bear it out. Where do we find freedom from guilt and frustration? No one will ever find freedom from guilt, emptiness, and futility except through Jesus Christ. For those who become Christians, the past is dead and buried with all its guilt and frustrations. Once we repent of our sin and accept by faith Jesus Christ, we are forgiven of everything. We truly are born again. We become a new creation (2 Corinthians 5:17). What a thought! That is revolutionary therapy. The most sin-stained life becomes white as snow (Isaiah 1:18). There is a land of beginning again. Where else but in Christ can we find a thorough cleansing of our conscience so that we are freed from the past? Can the doubter really discover a better freedom?

Where do we find freedom from fear? Again, only Christian believers possess true freedom from fear. An Atlanta television station scored a victory in its ratings war with competing stations when it broadcast a series of reports on fear. They honed in on a subject that touches us all. Everyone suffers from fear of one sort or another. We are frightened to think about life's possible eventualities — of becoming crippled, or losing those we love, or a thousand other possibilities. A million potential disasters haunt us.

However, as Christians who follow Christ, we know that He stands with us, waiting to help us in our struggles. He welcomes us into a totally new dimension of existence. If we keep our eyes on Jesus we can walk without sinking amidst the storms of life. To be thick-skinned and say we have no fear is simply a retreat from reality. No one is that strong—Nietzsche or anyone else. We are dependent creatures, like it or not. We must face facts. All are beset by fear. Therefore, can a truthful skeptic face his own future without a subtle dread, born of his own sense of nihilism? Can he really convince himself fully that he will not have to answer to God? One seriously doubts it. But there is help.

The Word of God states, "For God hath not given us the spirit of fear; but of power, and of love, and of a sound mind" (2 Timothy 1:7, KJV*). What a powerful truth to internalize and live and share.

Where do we find freedom from overpowering temptations? Sin is always "crouching at the door" (Genesis 4:7). Guilt over the past and fear of the future can easily enslave us, but the great threat to our freedom is the temptation of the moment.

To get hooked on bad attitudes and habits that are often all but impossible to overcome is very easy. In our battle with temptation, defeat often drives us to a point of helpless frustration. We just give up. The great Roman philosopher Seneca expressed his feelings of powerlessness: "I am in the grips of habits that enslave me! I cannot escape from the pits into which I have fallen unless an arm from above should rescue me."[6] Even the apostle Paul confessed,

> For that which I am doing, I do not understand; for I am not practicing what I would like to do, but I am doing the very thing I hate. . . . So now, no longer am I the one doing it, but sin which indwells me. For I know that nothing good dwells in me, that is, in my flesh; for the wishing is present in me, but the doing of the good is not. For the good that I wish, I do not do; but I practice the very evil that I do not wish. . . . Wretched man that I am! (Romans 7:15, 17-19, 24a.)

That gnawing feeling of helplessness can cause us to overcompensate. We try to convince ourselves that we are self-sufficient, self-made creatures who can shout out with pride and confidence: "We can do it!" But the result is an insecure conceitedness. Friedrich Nietzsche became so arrogant he finally said, "I have outgrown my need for God!" Did he? Can we? Can anyone? Of course not—not really. Christ alone can give us grace to overcome.

CONCLUSION

The entire scenario can be summed up in Jesus' own words: "If the Son sets you free, you will be free indeed" (John 8:36, NIV†). Jesus Christ alone gives true freedom and genuine personhood. Freedom does not rest in Nietzsche's concept of human self-sufficiency. That grows out of self-deception, if not satanic blindness. Selfhood comes in surrender to God. Our Lord said, "For whoever wishes to save his life shall lose it; but whoever loses his life for My sake and the gospel's shall save it" (Mark 8:35). Of course, becoming a Christian does not insure perfection. Believers still have struggles and sins. All have a long way to go. That we must grant. But believers are going in the right direction. In Christ we are becoming authentic selves.

* King James Version.
† New International Version.

6. Michael Green, Jesus Spells Freedom (London: Inter-Varsity, 1976), p. 29.

6

The Ridiculing Skeptic

I don't believe in God because I don't believe in Mother Goose.

— Clarence Darrow, lawyer (1857-1938)

THE RIDICULER AND HIS ARGUMENT

Clarence Darrow, the caustic critic of Christianity, earned a reputation for being one of the most astute lawyers and militant agnostics of modern times. He seemed to enjoy the bizarre. He was the man who represented the infamous child murderers Loeb and Leopold, the struggling labor leader Eugene Debs, and a small town schoolteacher accused of violating Tennessee's anti-evolution law. No doubt Darrow succeeded as a brilliant barrister. He defended over one hundred accused murderers and prevented the execution of every one.

Possessing a keen legal mind together with rare oratorical ability, he also displayed stunning and sensational audacity that cut across the grain of society's status quo regarding criminal rights, labor laws, race, and religion. Darrow was a thorough-going maverick who always stood on the side of the underdog, the criminal, the downtrodden, and even the godless. Much of what he said and did was commendable, but his sarcastic, ridiculing attacks on Christianity are quite unreasonable and, in the final analysis, indefensible.

Although we Christians are disturbed by ridiculing diatribes against our faith in Christ, Darrow's willingness to defend the losers in life is impressive — an admirable trait characteristic of the One we follow. After Darrow's stunning defense of eleven blacks arrested for defending themselves against a mob, Judge Frank Murphy turned to a friend and said, "This is the greatest experience in my life. That was Clarence Darrow at his best. I will never hear anything like it again. He is the most 'Christ-like' man I have ever known."[1]

At his best, Clarence Darrow was unquestionably one of the finest courtroom lawyers and social crusaders in American history. In the area of religion, however, he hardly displayed his best. That is evident in his well-known, but not well-argued article, "Why I Am an Agnostic." Although the work no doubt expressed his firm convictions, Darrow made several unfounded, dogmatic statements. For example, he said, "No one knows the time or the identity of any authors [of the biblical books]," and, "There can be no proof imagined that could be sufficient to show the violation of natural law [i.e., a miracle]."[2]

Of course, such statements are not true. A little serious research and thought expose their error. They are merely dogmatic declarations. Quite ironic is the fact that this man who forcefully attacked racial prejudice — an obvious Christian virtue — apparently found himself prejudiced against the Christian religion itself. He constructed a caricature of Christianity and then proceeded to attack it with condescending ridicule, assuming that it is immature and childish to believe in God. But, we must never forget, ridicule is always the weapon of weakness, not a convincing argument.

In Clarence Darrow's view, Christianity is for children. Explaining the reason for his stand, he declared, "I think that it is impossible for the human mind to believe in an object or thing unless it can form a mental picture of such an object or thing."[3] Therefore, Darrow saw the concept of God as silly, because one cannot form a mental picture of God. He explained his lack of belief by stating, "I don't believe in God

---

1. Houston Peterson, ed., *A Treasury of the World's Great Speeches* (New York: Simon and Schuster, 1965), p. 741.
2. Clarence Darrow, "Why I Am an Agnostic," *The Borzoi College Reader,* eds., Charles Muscatine and Marlene Griffith (New York: Knopf, 1971), p. 619.
3. Ibid., p. 618.

because I don't believe in Mother Goose."[4] In that statement he is reminiscent of the Greeks of Paul's day who called Christianity "foolishness" (1 Corinthians 1:23).

Darrow was not saying anything new. Christians have had to contend with that sort of ridicule for centuries. Therefore, believers should feel no serious threat. In reality, Darrow's charge creates the opportunity to present the Christian faith as something far more profound than Darrow and most ridiculers realize, something far removed from a fairy tale or foolishness. Christianity can be presented in a fashion that can be reasonably convincing to most any honest, open-minded juror or lawyer. In other words, a case can be built for Christianity against the charge of silliness.

AN ANSWER

It should first be acknowledged that in some cultures and religious systems there are immature ideas about God. That people will shave their heads, wear strange-looking clothes, and sing and dance in public as they proclaim their faith in the Hindu god Krishna does make some thinking people wonder at the validity of religion. That is not meant to ridicule other religions or religious people. They are often quite sincere. The sad part comes when one discovers their doctrines; for example, the belief system of the followers of Krishna. The Hindu scriptures portray their god as something of a playboy-warrior who, not satisfied with his sixteen thousand wives, lured married women and young girls from their families in order to become his lovers. What a perverted concept of a deity!

Another case in point is the religion of Africa's pygmies. One of the most important religious items among one pygmy tribe was an old drainpipe. They used it as a trumpet to blow when their god supposedly fell asleep. When sickness or famine occurred, they felt their god was slumbering and they must wake him.

There are many childish ideas in religion — that we must honestly grant. Even some professing Christians seem to hold immature ideas about God. A Harvard professor confessed that as a boy, growing up in a Christian home, he pictured God as a venerable bookkeeper with a white flowing beard,

4. George Seldes, comp., *The Great Quotations* (New York: Pocket Books, 1967), p. 418.

standing behind a high desk writing down everybody's bad deeds. He outgrew that shallow concept. Tragically, some do not. A late well-known New York pastor told of a young man who came to his study one day to announce he did not believe in God. "Tell me about the God you do not believe in," said the pastor. "Well," the young man answered, "I do not believe in a God who. . . ." And then he told all the bad things he thought of God. The pastor retorted, "I do not believe in that God either."

J. B. Phillips wrote a classic book attacking this problem entitled *Your God Is Too Small.* In it he discusses many of the inadequate ideas that some well-meaning Christians hold about God. All of that we must admit and attempt to correct. But the issue is: What is the *genuine* Christian understanding of God?

That leads us to an essential question: Is there a mature and sensible picture of God that can refute the charge of foolishness and put to rest the superficial ridicule of the Darrow-type skeptic? Can we present a picture of God that does not come over like a fairy tale? Christians do not believe in Mother Goose. But we do believe in Someone.

A problem surfaces when one attempts to describe God. John 1:18 states, "No one has seen God at any time." That means God is not subject to empirical (sense perception) investigation. You cannot put God in a test tube and examine Him. "God is Spirit" (John 4:24). In other words, God as Spirit is vastly different from us, not just in degree, but in essential kind. In His essence God defies human, empirical, rational description. Nevertheless, mankind seems bent to try to explain Him fully on these limited humanistic terms. That is the root of idolatry.

Many religions of the world are made up of sense perception guesses and human rationalistic ideas about God. And as implied, these ideas are often so humanistic and superficial, they are obviously false, if not idolatrous. They may even at times appear downright foolish, as idolatry always tends to be. We can be sure that the Creator of this vast, complex, and magnificent universe is not a childish playboy like Krishna. Nor is He a god who needs to be awakened by a drainpipe trumpet, and He certainly is not an old man with a white beard. If God is like that, then the whole Christian scheme really is silly. Deep down inside their personhood, people simply *know* that there are some things God cannot be. Yet,

He must be something. But we cannot see Him. How then can we know what God is like in order to dispel the Darrow myth?

It reduces itself to this: Although we must employ limited human language and thought in describing God, and though we can form at least some valid ideas of what God is like, because of our humanity and its limitations we are finally dependent on God to tell us who He is and what He is like. We can conceive a certain amount of the characteristics of God; nature reveals some of His attributes. As the Bible says, "The heavens are telling of the glory of God; and their expanse is declaring the work of His hands" (Psalm 19:1). But the point is, if we are to know God *truly and personally*, He must make Himself known. We dare not rely on human observation and conjecture alone. We simply cannot scale some rational mountain up into fellowship with God. He must come to us and show Himself. That is absolutely vital if we are to know God in any intimate, personal way — and that is what matters.

Now we Christians believe God has done just that. We believe He has unveiled Himself in clear and unmistakable terms. He has *revealed* Himself truly. Therefore, through God's revelation of Himself we can come to know Him and, as far as humanly possible, understand Him. (A full argument for the validity of revelation is found in chapter ten.) And how has He revealed Himself? In John 14:8-9 we read, "Philip said to Him, 'Lord, show us the Father, and it is enough for us.' Jesus said to him, 'Have I been so long with you, and yet you have not come to know Me, Philip? *He who has seen Me has seen the Father.*'" In the same vein, Paul writes in Colossians 1:15, Jesus is "the image of the invisible God."

Conclusion: Jesus Christ reveals the essence of God's character. Simply put, *Jesus is what God is like.* When we study the birth, life, death, and resurrection of Jesus Christ there is nothing more to be said, at least as far as we human beings can understand God. (It can be argued that the Jewish people knew much of God *before* Jesus Christ. That is true, but the Old Testament came primarily by *revelation*, and Jesus fulfilled it all. The principle of revelation is always at the heart of God — in any age.) Moreover, those historical facts are anything but foolish; they present a life-size, sensible, acceptable image of the God who reveals Himself.

THE BIRTH, LIFE, DEATH, AND RESURRECTION OF JESUS CHRIST

The birth narrative of our Lord is a simple report about simple people which even the simplest person can understand. But being simple does not make it simplistic or superficial. It is a long way from a Mother Goose tale. It is a perfect story. If the almighty God wants to communicate with us as mere human beings, He must do it *simply* so that everyone can understand His message. It seems most logical that if the infinite God were to address us in our limited humanity, at least in any measure of depth, He would become human to do it. Actually, that principle appears virtually mandatory. How could God Almighty speak to humanity unless He, in some sense, became human? That is the point the astute German philosopher Rudolph Otto makes in his classic book *The Idea of the Holy*. Moreover, He must do it *gently* so that we will not be overwhelmed. Consequently, God's Son, Jesus Christ, laid aside His splendor and came to earth as the Babe of Bethlehem. The Son came as a gentle child.

The birth account dramatically pictures the almighty God emptying Himself and slipping simply and gently into the stream of human history in order to alter the course of human events, yet without destroying human liberty or dignity. He did not burst in with all His glory and thus overawe us. He came as a human to speak to us on our level. That is truly tremendous, and just because the message is simple, that certainly does not negate its profundity. Actually, the biblical concept of the incarnation is the most profound and sublime thought the human mind can grapple with. The world's astute secular philosophers could hardly conceive of such a beautiful reality. Such revelational communication is a far cry from childish or foolish; on the contrary, it is most mature and unbelievably wise. We need to know God. Further, we need to feel emotionally that God truly cares for us. That is exactly what the incarnation accomplished. All of those and a thousand other marvelous concepts are wrapped up in the manger stall.

An illustration will help here. Over three hundred years ago Abbas the Great, the Shah of Persia, would frequently disguise himself in order to mingle with ordinary people. Whenever he visited the public baths he would spend time with the old man who stoked the fires. They became friends. The disguised Shah would sit and chat with the old man. They would share their food, thoughts, and feelings.

One day the Shah revealed his true identity. He said, "I am the Shah. I have been with you often and have come to know and appreciate you. You are a good man. Ask whatever you desire and I will give it to you." The old fire-keeper said, "You have eaten my food, rejoiced when I rejoiced, wept when I wept, and shared my burdens. I want nothing but your continued friendship, concern, and understanding. All I want is someone who understands me as I am."

It is in that sense that the story of Christ's birth is so relevant. There is nothing childish or foolish about that.

Therefore, it can be concluded that the revelational biblical account of the incarnate Lord Jesus Christ, preceded by what God has revealed in the Old Testament, is adequate for us and is sensible. As already stressed, if God were to communicate with us, the most logical way would be simply by becoming a human being. Theoretically, it might not be the *only* way, but God saw fit to do it that way; thus we conclude it was the *best* way. That does not preclude God also speaking through the prophets and apostles. It simply points out that Jesus Christ is the *fullest* revelation of God as we know it.

The fundamental principle of communication is to put oneself where the other person is. Therefore, God is saying in the incarnation of Christ, "This is the way I communicate with you." The simple, yet profound, incarnation of Christ answers one of the basic questions as to the nature of God; He comes to us in love to reveal Himself.

The marvelous life of our incarnate Lord makes the whole revelational principle even more convincing. Jesus lived the most revolutionary and irrefutably good life the world has ever seen. No one seriously denies that. Moreover, there is simply no natural humanistic explanation for it. The historical evidence of Jesus' life surely points to the fact that He had to be divine. Comparative religious studies show how utterly different Jesus was from all other spiritual leaders. At the age of thirty He began an earth-changing ministry that lasted three years. Yet in those short days:

> He touched the untouchable lepers.
> He visited in the homes of sinners and outcasts.
> He healed people without asking anything in return.
> He spoke forcefully and prophetically yet always with under-

standing and compassion.
He condemned the evil in all of us but was willing to forgive
any and every sin.
He claimed to be God Almighty, yet had such overwhelming
humility.

Even the critical Goethe had to confess, "If ever the Divine
appeared on earth, it was in the Person of Christ."[5] His goodness was sublime. The world has seen many good people, but
not like Jesus of Nazareth. Michael Green summarizes the
awesome attractiveness of Jesus' perfect life when he writes,
"Nobody has been able to show any evil contained in it.
Nobody has been able to show any good not contained in it."[6]
Christ's whole life and dynamic teaching is a vivid demon-
stration of "God with us." What other conclusion is plausible,
except that Jesus truly was the unique Son of God and that
He came to show us the very nature of God? Therefore,
when people want to know what God is like, tell them Jesus is
what God is like. Surely that will eliminate much serious ridicule. One can hardly ridicule Him.

What is so astonishing about the Lord Jesus is that He
lived up completely to His fantastic claims and moral teachings. Jesus' own ethical life gives us an unquestionably mature
and wise picture of how to live and of how to understand
God in human affairs. One would have thought the whole
world would have hung on His every word. Yet, at the age of
thirty-three Jesus suffered crucifixion by selfish, self-centered,
cruel men. When one considers how He lived, the fact that
He was betrayed, tortured, and crucified defies imagination.

When we realize that we destroyed the greatest Person
who ever lived, we are forced to face the most glaring problem of human nature: sin. Our sinfulness crucified Jesus. Our
selfish rebellion nailed Him to the cross. Our pride pierced
His side.

Divine wisdom had prepared for and even planned the
events at Golgotha. The tragedy at Calvary provided the way
for Jesus to pay for our sin; sin manifested in the greed, hate,
prejudice, jealousy, injustice, and apathy of all mankind —
even good religious people. To deal with the problem of
human evil, Jesus died. He felt the full fury of our sin on the

5. Josh McDowell, *Evidence That Demands a Verdict* (San Bernardino,
   Calif.: Campus Crusade for Christ, 1972), p. 133.
6. Michael Green, *Jesus Spells Freedom* (London: Inter-Varsity, 1972), p. 47.

cross and saved us. The tragedy was transformed into glory. He could do that because He was man and yet different from all other men; He was the perfect Son of God. He stands in time *and* eternity, in the river of life and on the bank of eternity. He is, in a most mysterious yet marvelous way, the Friend who steps into the river and offers His hand. And He did it all in His vicarious, substitutionary death.

This simple, striking story of Calvary has touched the heart of multitudes. It has appealed to all peoples of all times and cultures. For example, when Christian missionaries first went to Clovis, king of the Franks, they told him how Jesus came, suffered, and died on Calvary. After they finished telling the king about Jesus Christ, the old monarch jumped up with tears in his eyes and with hand on his sword cried, "If I and my Franks had been there, we would have stormed Calvary and rescued Him from His enemies!"

Sophisticated intellectuals have been touched as well. Benjamin Franklin was never, as far as we know, an orthodox Christian. He had difficulty believing that Jesus was the Son of God. But shortly before Franklin died, he requested a picture of Jesus on the cross to be placed in his bedroom so he could look upon it.

Death did not have the final word for our Lord. On the third day He was gloriously resurrected, never to die again. His tomb is empty. *He is alive.* And we can live with Him. He was "raised because of our justification" (Romans 4:25). The resurrection is as vital to salvation and life as the cross. Christianity is the religion of the resurrection. The death and resurrection of Christ cut across all cultures and speak to all. He lives to aid, comfort, save, and forgive anyone who will look to Him. He is always there. What is childish or foolish about that?

CONCLUSION

When the ridiculer of the Darrow mind-set starts throwing accusations of the childishness of Christianity, point to Jesus. He is what God is like. You as a believer can stand on the life, death, and resurrection of the Lord Jesus Christ. Nothing flung at that foundation can move it. "We preach Christ crucified" (1 Corinthians 1:23). That is the gospel, and it is its own defense against the charge of foolishness. The gospel is the "power of God unto salvation" (Romans 1:16, KJV).

One day a young ministerial student came to the great nineteenth-century English preacher Charles Spurgeon and asked, "Mr. Spurgeon, how do you defend the gospel?"

"Defend the gospel!" Spurgeon exclaimed, "How do you defend a lion?" Obviously, you don't; you turn it loose. The gospel contains its own power; turn it loose!

7

The Political Activist Skeptic

I think all the great religions of the world [are] . . . both
untrue and harmful.
— Bertrand Russell, mathematician, philosopher,
political activist (1872-1970)

THE POLITICAL ACTIVIST SKEPTIC AND HIS ARGUMENT

The man who will always be known as the twentieth-
century symbol of the political activist skeptic is the British
thinker and philosopher Bertrand Russell. While still a small
child, Russell's parents died, leaving him in the guardianship
of two tutors. Both were atheists. Later, Russell's grandpar-
ents intervened to rescue their grandchildren "from the
clutches of intriguing infidels."[1] Their success, however, was
only temporary, for at the age of eighteen Bertrand Russell
became an outright atheist. Russell might well be described
as one of the most notorious and influential atheists of our
time. His philosophical system is studied far and wide. In his
book *Why I Am Not a Christian and Other Essays on Religion
and Related Subjects,* he clearly communicated his forthright
rejection of religion in general and Christianity in particular.

Russell, never deterred by how unpopular his positions

---

1. Bertrand Russell, *The Autobiography of Bertrand Russell, The Early
   Years: 1872-World War One* (New York: Bantam, 1969), p. 10.

might be, was a pacifist during World War I, forbidden to
teach at the City College of New York because of his outspoken ideas, which earned him a reputation for immorality,
and was imprisoned at the age of ninety as a result of his
disarmament demonstrations. While involved in peace
marches, he called John F. Kennedy one of the wickedest
men in history.[2]

That kind of notoriety should not obscure the fact that
Bertrand Russell was a gifted individual. He excelled as a
masterful mathematician and a provocative philosopher. His
Principia Mathematica is classic. He was also a dedicated lib-
eral crusader. The humanitarian heart of Bertrand Russell is
most deserving of respect. In his autobiography he wrote
words that reflect this genuine concern for humanity: "Children in famine, victims tortured by oppressors, helpless old
people a hated burden to their sons and the whole world of
loneliness, poverty, and pain make a mockery of what human
life should be. I love to alleviate the evil, but I cannot, and I
too suffer."[3]

Russell's problem seemed to be that he believed that
neither Christianity nor any other religion helped to alleviate
human suffering. He even felt religion impeded progress.
That was one of his most serious objections to faith in God.
He went so far as to declare that "all the great religions of the
world . . . [are] both untrue and harmful."[4] He stated
categorically,

> Every single bit of progress in human feeling, every improve-
> ment in the criminal law, every step toward diminution of
> war, every step toward better treatment of the colored races,
> and every mitigation of slavery, every moral progress that
> there has been in the world, has been consistently opposed by
> the organized churches of the world. I say quite deliberately
> that the Christian religion, as organized in its churches, has
> been and still is the principal enemy of moral progress in the
> world.[5]

In an article entitled "Has Religion Made Useful Contributions to Civilization?" Russell answered his own question by

2. Christopher Booker, *The Neophiliacs* (Boston: Gambit, 1970), p. 171.
3. Russell, p. 4.
4. Bertrand Russell, *Why I Am Not a Christian and Other Essays on Religion and Related Subjects* (New York: Simon and Schuster, 1957), p. v.
5. Ibid., pp. 20-21.

stating that religion has made only two contributions to civilization: helping to establish a calendar and predict eclipses. That is all. "I do not know of any others," he said.[6]

Bertrand Russell became convinced that religion is a regressive force that seeks to maintain the status quo. His basic argument stated that religion always appeared as a defender of what is, rather than a promoter of what ought to be. Therefore, religion should be eliminated.

If Russell's caustic comments are true, then we should all probably join in to tear down the tenets of religious faith. However, is his analysis accurate? We Christians disagree with Russell's conclusions, of course. But what can be said to those who see religion as a mere defender of the status quo, having no desire, let alone a strategy, to meet the pressing need of change to better humanity's lot? In a word, how do we respond to those who think Christianity has nothing to offer to cure the desperate social and political ills of our day? What do we say to people who see Christians as interested only in "pie in the sky," thus unconcerned with real life?

AN ANSWER

First, let us grant—as we have had to do in other areas—that some world religions actually are defenders of the status quo. We must further acknowledge that at times even certain Christian churches and individual believers are stagnant, resting in the status quo, defending the undefendable. As an instance, Leighton Ford describes the tragic and pathetic case of the Russian Orthodox church: "While revolution was raging in Petrograd in 1917, the Russian Orthodox church was in session a few blocks away reportedly having a warm debate about what color vestments their priests should wear! God help us if we are straining at gnats while the camels of revolution are marching!"[7]

The Constantine church was no sterling example of true Christianity either. To admit our own sins and shortcomings is necessary before we can convincingly communicate with the critic. The church has often quite seriously failed. But mature Christianity is not to be seen in those churches or

6. Ibid., p. 24.
7. Leighton Ford, *One Way to Change the World* (New York: Harper and Row, 1970), p. 13.

individuals who defend the evils of their contemporary
society. True Christianity as Jesus Christ presented it is a
forward-looking, mind-stretching, radical movement. Faith as
designed by the Lord Jesus Christ is revolutionary, offering
people and society a whole new way of life. We should all
join the cry of Leighton Ford who said, "God [gave] . . . us
courage to be like the prophets who climbed their watch-
towers to see what God was doing in the world . . . we need a
holy discontent with the status quo. The Gospel calls for constant change. In that sense we are radicals."[8]

Jesus Himself was never caught standing still. He was the
most positive, progressive personality the world has ever
known. Jesus declared, "I have come to cast fire upon the
earth; and how I wish it were already kindled!" (Luke 12:49).
He ignited the fires of thorough revival and renewal in which
people and society can be radically changed. This does not
mean Jesus was a destructive revolutionary. To the contrary,
He worked as a revolutionary builder of a better life and
society. And just because the church has at times failed, that
does not negate true Christianity.

Furthermore, the church at its best has always realized and
practiced this principle. In its finest hours it forsook the comfortable pew and got out on the battlefield. History attests to
success as well as failure. Chapter 2 of Acts records how the
first Christian believers experienced the spirit of revival and
became God's revolutionary change agents. Our Lord designed the church at its very inception to be a promoter of
what ought to be. And in countless cases the church has risen
to its challenge. The record of the true Body of Christ
through the centuries refutes much of Bertrand Russell's
argument. Actually, the church has made countless outstanding positive and progressive contributions to civilization. Christians have led the fight against our greatest social and individual problems in spite of those who want to defend the old,
worn-out traditions of a decaying social order. A multitude of
examples can be presented.

THE PROBLEM OF DISEASE

There have always been efforts to help the sick, yet after
the founding of the Christian church, hospitals were estab-

---

8.   Ibid., p. 13.

lished in numbers as never before witnessed in history. The word *hospital* is a Latin derivation originally meaning a "Christian guest house" for sick, weary, homeless travelers. Christians became the great pioneers in fighting disease as they tried to follow in the footsteps of Jesus who came as Savior and *Healer*. When Christians see how Jesus healed every imaginable kind of sickness, they know they must follow His lead. Through the years the Christian church has sent thousands upon thousands of willing volunteers to the remotest places on earth to deal with every sort of disease.

THE PROBLEM OF POVERTY

Jesus said that poverty would always be a problem in our world. The abundance of self-indulgent greed and the scarcity of self-sacrificing generosity make it so. But by His teachings and example, Jesus attacked both the symptoms and causes of poverty. He came as Savior and *Social Worker*.

The early Christian church followed the Lord by forthrightly addressing the poverty problem. Acts 2:44-45 states, "And all those who had believed were together, and had all things in common; and they began selling their property and possessions, and were sharing them with all, as anyone might have need." These generous Christians earned a matchless reputation for taking care of widows, orphans, and the handicapped. And it did not end in the first century.

Bertrand Russell gave the impression that Christians have done virtually nothing to care for the poor. That is simply not true. Any objective study of history demonstrates the error. The church has always been, to a greater or lesser degree, the traditional and dependable friend of the poor and oppressed whom seemingly everyone else turned away. There are a few dark spots to be sure, but generally that is true.

Granted, the church has not been perfect, but atheists like Bertrand Russell and Karl Marx point out only the times of failures. They almost seem to enjoy mentioning the plight of English men, women, and children who were exploited during the Industrial Revolution while, as they say, many church leaders did very little to help. But that is not the whole story. Both Russell and Marx ignore the facts that historians like Green, Lecky, and Trevelyan freely admit: In the eighteenth and nineteenth century Christian revivals gave birth to magnificent Christian-led social reforms that prevented violent revolutions in England.[9] Christians like Charles Wesley, William Wilberforce, Lord Shaftesbury, William Booth, George Williams, and a host of others became the pioneering social reformers who fought for the poor and were significantly successful in achieving help for the downcast and underprivileged. Prison reforms, public education,and labor laws were changed because of their efforts. George Sweazer writes,

> Lord Shaftesbury, an evangelical [Christian] . . . expressed his faith through sixty years of public life that were dedicated to social reform. No other leader of Parliament ever did as much to secure legislation which improved the condition of industrial workers. His real constituents were the laborers in mines, farms, and factories, the insane, chimney sweeps, women, children, and slum dwellers.[10]

Actually, Christians launched the first great war on poverty in our Industrial Age.

THE PROBLEM OF PREJUDICE

Class prejudice is always with us. Clannish, small-minded prejudice abounds all over the world. True Christianity is dead set against it. Galatians 3:28 tells us, "There is neither Jew nor Greek, there is neither slave nor free man, there is neither male nor female; for you are all one in Christ Jesus." There is no place for prejudice in the kingdom of God. All Christians need to rid their lives of it and proclaim acceptance of all in Christ. Jesus came as Savior and *Unifier*. He brings us together.

That is the miracle of true Christianity. And even if some Christians fail right there, it is not Christianity's failure. Nor have all failed by any means. Countless Christians have crossed cultural, racial, and language barriers because they have learned to cross one of the greatest barriers of all — prejudice. What other religion or philosophy has so highly motivated people to fight with such fervor against their own prejudice?

THE PROBLEM OF SLAVERY

Surely there is nothing more dehumanizing than slavery.

9. George Sweazer, *The Church As Evangelist* (New York: Harper and Row, 1978), p. 23.
10. Ibid., p. 24.

As Christians we must remember that Christ came as Savior and *Liberator.* The early Christians treated slaves as brothers and sisters; for that is what they were. Ultimately, that spelled the end of slavery.

When the slave trade flourished in Africa, many Christian leaders took a strong stand against the insidious evil — Christians like missionary David Livingstone, evangelist Charles Finney, and pastor Charles Spurgeon. John Newton, a slave trader, found Christ on a slave ship on the high seas. He eventually forsook slave trading, became a pastor, and wrote "Amazing Grace." While the Moslem religion endorsed slavery, while economic interests profited from it, while politicians ignored it, more than a few Christians declared war against it. The track record was far from perfect, but many Christians led the way.

Wilberforce led the fight to outlaw slavery throughout the British empire. He entered politics in 1780. Five years later he was converted and became a forceful Christian politician who earned the reputation of being the conscience of the British people. He delivered one of the greatest and longest speeches in Parliamentary history. Wilberforce spoke in Parliament well over three hours as he described the vileness and shame of slavery. He challenged men of conscience to rise up and wipe out the curse. Wilberforce and other Christians waged a holy war against one of the unholiest practices known to human history. Theodore Weld, a fervent evangelical Christian, led the fight in America. Christians pointed the way.

THE PROBLEM OF IGNORANCE

Jesus stressed the importance of education; He is known as Savior and *Teacher.* Jesus not only taught men but women and children also. That was revolutionary in itself. Jesus challenged all people to think differently and deeply. He became an educator par excellence. He instructed His disciples to teach others as He had taught them (Matthew 28:19-20). Actually, He was best known as a teacher.

Christians have built the first schools in many parts of the world. As a result of the great nineteenth-century spiritual awakening in America, literally hundreds of colleges and schools were founded.

Bertrand Russell and like-minded skeptics would have us

believe that Christianity wants ignorant people. Russell charged that Christianity is both unscientific and anti-science. Some Christians may have given Russell ammunition for his guns; yet, Christianity stands as an education-oriented faith. Christians have often led the way in broadening and deepening the human mind as well as the human spirit.

THE PROBLEM OF WAR

Bertrand Russell fought as a leading pacifist and active demonstrator. He argued that the Christian church had done more to support war than to stop it. That is not true. Remember, Jesus came as Savior and *Prince of Peace.* Unlike the Islamic religion, Christianity, rightly understood, declares war on war, pronouncing war as being unholy and barbaric, even if history shows some serious shortcomings on the part of some professing believers.

Adolf Hitler created a hell for the Jews and those Christians who dared to oppose him. When we divorce ourselves from God we end up in some sort of hell, sooner or later. That kind of judgment is our own creation. We cannot blame God or the Christian faith because it occurs in a so-called Christian nation. The fact is, through lust, people can be utterly self-destructive. That is why wars occur. Christianity teaches and history confirms that war and other forms of conflict originate in the violent hearts of people who have shut the Prince of Peace out of their lives (James 4:1).

As sensible Christians and responsible citizens, we know that peace marches and unilateral disarmament alone will never achieve real peace on earth in our time or anyone else's. Neville Chamberlain tried it in the 1930s, but he only succeeded in allowing Hitler to expand his reign of terror. The one and only solution to the problem of war lies in *change of heart.* Christianity addresses this most pressing problem and offers the only change of heart that can save — save one from self-centeredness and eventual self-destructiveness.

That does not mean Christians should not go all out to eradicate the scourge of war in a national, political sense. But the only assurance of peace comes through the power of Jesus Christ to change people and society. If that is not a contribution to civilization, what is? Christians have led the way in demonstrating how we can overcome war, whether it is on the battlefield, in the home, or in the mind itself. Christians know the way that leads to the "peace of God, which surpasses all comprehension" (Philippians 4:7). Russell missed that essential truth.

CONCLUSION

When Jesus came to earth, history was divided into B. C. and A. D. He came to change the status quo. The reverberations of His coming are still being felt. He is still working through the lives of His change-agents. Let no one say that Christianity has made no contribution to the well-being of society and should be written off. It is not so.

Do not be taken in by the skeptical argument and hence become defenseless in the face of half-truth accusations. Learn the facts. Study history. See all the benefits the church has made. Christians can hold their heads high concerning their involvement in bettering this world. We must learn our history and always be ready to defend our faith.

8

The Christian Skeptic

It's no longer possible for Western man to know [experience] the transcendent God.

—Thomas Altizer, "Christian" atheist (1927)

THE CHRISTIAN ATHEIST AND HIS ARGUMENT

Of all the skeptics and their systems discussed thus far, none is more intriguing—and puzzling—than Thomas J. J. Altizer. He and his followers profess to be *Christian* atheists. Altizer is known as the "most widely advertised representative of the 'death of God' group."[1] We expect an atheist like Friedrich Nietzsche, "who prided himself on being the anti-Christ,"[2] to announce the death of God; but it is unexpected and almost unbelievable to hear an Episcopalian theologian, formally teaching in a Methodist university in the heart of the Bible Belt, say, "It is precisely the acceptance of Nietzsche's proclamation of the death of God that is the real test of a contemporary form of faith."[3] Listening to Altizer, by implication, identifying Nietzsche as a Christian and himself

1. Roch A. Kereszty, *God Seekers for a New Age* (Dayton, Ohio: Pflaum, 1970), p. 38.
2. Thomas W. Ogletree, *The Death of God Controversy* (Nashville: Abingdon, 1966), p. 79.
3. Thomas J. J. Altizer and William Hamilton, *Radical Theology and the Death of God* (New York: Bobbs-Merrill, 1966), p. 11.

as a Christian atheist is both fascinating and bewildering. But that is exactly what he does.

The title of Thomas Altizer's book *The Gospel of Christian Atheism* expresses his conviction that not only is God dead, but this is good news; it is a fact to celebrate. Whether Altizer's announcement is considered good or bad news, his ideas made news headlines. And although they are no longer center-page in the secular press, they are still, to a greater or lesser degree, shared by many. His complete secularizing of the gospel has appeal to many a secular-oriented skeptic.

Since leaving Methodist-founded Emory University in 1968, Altizer has been teaching at the State University of New York. Although he propounded his concept some years ago, a recent newspaper article in *The Atlanta Journal* noted that Altizer has not changed his views. They are still being expressed by him and others who have followed in his footsteps.[4] Moreover, Altizer believes that his radical teachings are so well entrenched that they are no longer threatened by evangelical or fundamentalistic Christianity. He states condescendingly, "Few of them [evangelical-fundamentalist Christians] have any brains."[5]

Who is this Christian atheist? Thomas W. Ogletree writes, "Altizer has been described as a 'profane mystic,' and as an 'apocalyptic prophet'; his writings are 'pure poetry,' beautiful but unintelligible."[6] John Warwick Montgomery depicts him as a "mortician-mystic."[7] Thomas Altizer might best be labeled as a man of his secular age, a religious radical whose revolutionary ideas seem to belong to the turbulent sixties when tradition was out and innovation in. He claims to speak on behalf of modern people whom he feels have lost their sense of God. He is a pure secularist trying to speak to a secular world that lost its transcendental grip on God. He grants God may have existed at one time, but now that man has come of age God died, and secularism reigns alone. The "Secular City" has arrived. His approach is a complete and radical secularization of the gospel. All the transcendental elements of Christianity are sloughed off. He feels he must do this to

4. Jim Galloway, *The Atlanta Journal*, 15 August 1982.
5. Ibid.
6. Ogletree, p. 75.
7. John Warwick Montgomery, *The "Is God Dead?" Controversy* (Grand Rapids: Zondervan, 1966), p. 21.

make Christianity sensible and compatible to modern, secular society.

This mortician-theologian argues that "God has died in our cosmos, in our history, in our existence."[8] His fundamental starting point appears to be that, "It's no longer possible for Western man to know the transcendent God as a source of life and joy."[9] The full-bloom secular age is here. Shout for joy! We need a transcendent God no more. We are of age at last. Nietzsche lamented God's death; Altizer rejoices for now that we are of age, we can well do without Him. Altizer says that "the only reality we know is the world of darkness."[10] He is convinced that we can neither "know the reality of God's presence nor understand the world as His creation."[11] The transcendental is gone; secularity permeates all reality.

That argument for Christian atheism is spelled out by another radical theologian, William Hamilton. He explains, "We are not talking about the absence of the experience of God, but about the experience of the absence of God."[12] Without trying to unravel in detail the twisted bundles of the death of God theology (which is linked to the thought of Sigmund Freud, Friedrich Nietzsche, and G. F. W. Hegel), it is not an oversimplification to say that the root of Christian atheism is found in the secular soil of scholars seemingly not experiencing God's presence in their lives. So they tell us God is dead. But how then can they claim to be Christian? The answer is simple; they retain the *ethics* and *moral example* of Jesus, but reject His metaphysics. That may be oversimplifying it somewhat, yet that is the essence of the issue. They want to make Jesus' moral teaching relevant to life as they see it. Thus they call themselves Christian. The rest, the transcendental metaphysics, they simply throw away, so they call themselves atheists. True, Altizer has his own metaphysics, but they are of a non-theistic, mystical sort. The whole scheme tends to be a secular humanism in religious ethical garb. The end result is a Christian-atheism, if the two terms can be legitimately combined.

It must be made clear here that not all secular skeptics are nearly as radical as Hamilton and Altizer. Some just say they

8. Altizer and Hamilton, p. 21.
9. *The Altizer-Montgomery Dialogue* (Chicago: InterVarsity, 1967), p. 86.
10. Ibid., p. 58.
11. Altizer and Hamilton, p. 95.
12. Ibid., p. 28.

have sought God and cannot find Him. They are more humble in their statements on the actual existence of God.

Now we must be always sympathetic to honest doubters, as strange as they may seem to us who believe. Moreover, at times we all have our own problems, and thus we should see ourselves as fellow strugglers. But still we must have a word for those who have not experienced God, whether they be radical like Altizer or more humble like many other secular-humanists.

AN ANSWER

Much that has been outlined in previous chapters is sound reason for rejecting secular humanism. And there is another line to take. It may appear overly subjective, yet it is grounded in the objective reality of God and His promise.

The argument begins by taking seriously for ourselves and suggesting seriously to the skeptic the objective biblical invitation, "O taste and see that the Lord is good" (Psalm 34:8). God invites all people to take the faith test, to conduct a spiritual experiment and find out for oneself if He really is alive. He promises that those who seek Him will find Him: "You will find Him if you search for Him *with all your heart*" (Deuteronomy 4:29, italics added). God really means it. If we truly seek God wholeheartedly the experiment will not fail— even if Altizer seems to doubt it.

There are sound reasons for accepting that invitation and seeing for oneself whether or not God is dead. First, there is the subtle but very real universal spiritual hunger for God. Second, the testimony of others concerning the reality of God stands in bold relief. Third, there is the problem of atheism concerning social well-being. All three testify to the reality and existence of God. Even though we all struggle, there is a God who responds to our seeking. Look at these three realities in more depth.

PEOPLE'S SPIRITUAL INCLINATION

Psalm 42:1-2 describes humanity's deep rooted hunger to know God: So my soul pants for Thee, O God. My soul thirsts for God, for the living God.

As we discovered in chapter 2, we are creatures who want to know our Creator, as children desire to know their parents. Whether a person will acknowledge it or not, we are religious beings seeking answers to problems that only God in Christ can give.

For example, we desire goodness, but the best of us have some of the worst in us: "All have sinned, and come short of the glory of God" (Romans 3:23, KJV). Even the crass skeptic who denies the reality of sin, commits it and experiences guilt. How then do we find forgiveness for our sins and power to overcome future temptations? Only God through Jesus Christ can resolve that universal problem. Hence, the innate desire to know Him personally is always there, subtle as it may be.

We all are aware of our need to love and be loved. But how often have people found a love that can outshine the darkness of hate? Is there a love that never grows old and cold? There is; God is love. To know Him in His love is life's greatest goal, and we all inwardly sense that and hence crave Him, realize it or not.

The glad and hearty affirmation to all these and a thousand more pressing human needs is Jesus Christ—the ultimate answer to the human dilemma. Even the most skeptical must admit that Jesus has a wonderful magnetic appeal. An open-minded Hindu put it well: "There is no one else seriously bidding for the heart of the world except Jesus Christ."[13]

There is simply something in us all that draws us to Jesus. The point is: Jesus by His Spirit stimulates the spiritual inclination of the sincere seeker. We believers can rightly assume that and build our witness on it, for this spiritual inclination is everywhere, even in personalities like the well-known existentialist and atheist, Jean-Paul Sartre. He confessed that he once had experienced the presence of God, but he chose to resist God, suppress his Godward urge, and thus become a full-fledged atheist.[14]

What a mistake to reject the seeking God when He reveals Himself! God's appeal touches the innermost nerve of all. Yet, the right to resist that appeal is our God-given privilege. We are created with freedom. Sartre exercised that right, thus opting to suppress rather than express his religious instincts. Many have seemingly chosen to suppress their innate inclination and hunger for God, thus preempting any openness to

13. E. Stanley Jones, *The Way* (New York: Doubleday, 1978), p. 24.
14. Jean-Paul Sartre, *The Words* (New York: George Braziller, 1964), pp. 102-3.

God as revealed in the historic Jesus. Remember, an atheist is
an atheist by his own choosing, not the lack of God speaking
to and seeking him.

THE TESTIMONY OF OTHERS

Altizer and Hamilton not only apparently suppress their
own spiritual instincts as God reveals Himself, they also
rather summarily dismiss the testimony of others concerning
the reality of God in their lives. Such a course is certainly not
wise. The testimony of countless millions through the ages
clearly points to the reality of God. The psalmist, even in the
midst of his enemies, is able to say, "This I know, that God is
for me" (Psalm 56:9). At the end of his excruciating ordeal
Job was able to say, "I have heard of Thee by the hearing of
the ear; but now my eye sees Thee" (Job 42:5). God is there
right in the midst of life, in its joys and in its pain. Job had
begun by believing God, but now he had come to know Him
in a personal way. Can we accept the testimonies of the
psalmist and Job? Yes, because they are reinforced by the
fact that they and a multitide of others are trustworthy
people.

A mere cursory survey of history clearly demonstrates that
reliable people of every age and culture have had unmistakable, genuine religious experiences. What is particularly impressive is that we have well-documented testimonies from
intelligent, well-balanced, and believable individuals. How
could so many be so wrong?

True, the argument from religious experience does not
incontestably prove God, but to simply ignore such a mountain of evidence is hardly honest investigation. It just cannot
be so easily set aside as the secularists might have us believe.

Blaise Pascal was one of the world's greatest physicists and
mathematicians, one of the world's finest scientists. He became absolutely convinced that God was not only alive, but a
living part of his life. He compared his encounter with God's
Spirit to a fire. God's fire had warmed his heart, enlightened
his mind, and set his conscience on fire. It is an inner revolution, testified Pascal. Is he not a reasonable witness for
Christianity?

C. S. Lewis is perhaps the most logical twentieth-century
defender of the faith. He was an atheist before being converted to Christ. His move toward a Christian conversion

reached a critical point while he was riding a bus. He suddenly realized that he was suppressing spiritual realities and his own hunger for God. He knew he had to make a choice: whether or not to open his mind, heart, and soul to the God who truly does confront people. As he faced that choice, he saw that his life was a "zoo of lusts, bedlam of ambition, a nursery of fears, and harem of fouled hates."[15]

Lewis turned to God with all his heart and discovered that God works wonders in *yielded* people's lives. C. S. Lewis, professor of English literature at Oxford and then Cambridge, went on to become a literary evangelist for Jesus Christ, proclaiming that anyone can find new life in Christ and know God in a deep and personal way if they will yield to Him. That is the issue; the seeker must be willing to yield to God as he seeks Him with all his heart. Surrender finds the Savior.

When the death of God theology was making news, Billy Graham was interviewed on the NBC-TV news show "Today." Being asked how he knew God was not dead, Graham replied, "Because I spoke to Him this morning." That is not a glib or shallow answer. It is a testimony based on genuine religious experience. It can, of course, be rejected, but it cannot be refuted. One simply cannot prove Graham did not talk with God. Millions of sensible, honest Christians *know* He is alive.

SOCIAL IMPROVEMENTS THROUGH CHRIST

Remember Jesus' healing of the blind man? The religious leaders who were opposing the Lord tried to discredit the report of that healing, but the blind man did not falter under their cross-examination. He declared, "One thing I do know that whereas I was blind, now I see" (John 9:25). Someone else has said:

> One thing we know: The most successful cure for alcoholism and every other drug addiction is a personal experience with Jesus Christ.
> One thing we know: The most successful defense against family disaster is having a home where people follow Christ.
> One thing we know: The most successful therapy for emotional troubles is rooted in a relationship with Christ.

15. C. S. Lewis, *Surprised by Joy* (New York: Harcourt, Brace and World, 1955), p. 226.

> One thing we know: The most successful solution to social
> evils is a spiritual revival where people feel the full impact of
> God's love in their lives.

Who could come into a dynamic experience of Jesus Christ
and fail to be a better person? Granted, there is much superficial Christianity today. There always has been and probably
always will be. But surely, a *true* experience of Christ always
changes life for the better. All society benefits from genuine
Christian experience.

Both Thomas Altizer and William Hamilton declare that we
can create a better world if we are divorced from traditional,
transcendental Christianity. That has been the basic argument of secular humanists of all stripes for hundreds of
years. The attitude can be traced back to the Tower of Babel.
Are they right?

Harold J. Brown, professor of law at Harvard University
Law School, states that separation from our traditional religious values has brought us to the point where "our whole
culture seems to be facing the possibility of a nervous break-
down."[16] The secular skeptic should be reminded of that sad
truth. And just to say, as they might, that they are not giving
up the *ethics* or *morals* of Christianity will never do. No one
can live out the ethics of Jesus without the transcendental
experience of knowing Jesus personally in religious experience, because that is where the *power* to live out Christian
morality is found. Moral precepts alone will not do. They
must be lived out in life.

Contemporary writers who have chosen to experience nothing but the absence of God have tended to produce novels
and dramas that are preoccupied with violence, immorality,
perversion, and self-destructiveness. There are few real heroes
— healthy and happy characters. There are exceptions, of
course, but the general rule holds. Atheism is always ultimately destructive, despite its claim to hold on to morals.
Even Thomas Altizer admitted that the God is dead philosophy could possibly lead to "madness and dehumanization"
and "moral chaos and life destroying nihilism."[17] If that is
true, even remotely — as Altizer admits — it seems a total

16. Harold J. Brown, *Christianity Today* (27 March 1981), p. 42.
17. Vernon C. Grounds, *Is God Dead?* (Grand Rapids: Zondervan, 1966),
    p. 55.

mystery that he and his disciples embrace the atheistic stand so enthusiastically. Truth should always produce good, not evil. That basic logic is somehow overlooked or ignored or forgotten in a humanistic secular philosophy of life.

Even a casual look at the atheistic political philosophies, which have materialized in dominant fashion throughout much of our contemporary world, reveals a frightening scenario of a morality characterized by Altizer's own phrases. The devastating dangers associated with any kind of "God is dead" way of thinking and living is spelled out in Fyodor Dostoyevsky's classic novel *The Brothers Karamasov.* In a conversation with the murderer of his father, Ivan, the avowed atheist is shocked and shaken when told that he and his atheistic viewpoint gave Smerdyakov, the murderer, the license to kill. The murderer explained that he had learned from Ivan that since God was dead or nonexistent all things were lawful: "Smerdyakov articulated in a shaking voice. . .'Everlasting God, there's no such thing as virtue, and there's no need of it. You were right. So that's how I looked at it.' "[18]

Dostoyevsky reminds us not to be shocked by what we read in the newspapers concerning what is happening at the hands of God-denying people. When God is taken out of a society and pure secularism reigns, even a quest for the Christian morality dies, and anarchy finally rules.

Such bad news should convince anyone to conduct the spiritual experiment of faith, take the faith test, and see how good the good news actually is. With the living Christ there is hope for a better world and life. Without the Lord, what is left? "In Him all things hold together" (Colossians 1:17).

CONCLUSION

Thus we are back to the basis of Christianity: Jesus Christ. He is not dead. He fulfills the innate longing for God. The testimony of the ages is valid. He makes the difference between chaos and a viable society. He lives and will reveal Himself to the true seeker.

18. Fyodor Dostoyevsky, *The Brothers Karamasov,* trans. Constance Garnett (New York: Random, 1950), pp. 768-69.

9

The Deist Skeptic

I believe in God, not the God of the mystics and the theologians, but the God of nature, the great geometrician, the architect of the universe, the prime mover, unalterable, transcendental, everlasting.

Voltaire (Francois Marie Arouet), philosopher (1694-1778)

THE DEIST AND HIS ARGUMENT

A professor writing to a minister-friend stated, "There are scads of students I have discovered on our university campuses that are, in the final analysis, Deistic. . .believing in a 'force' beyond it all, but a quite *impersonal* 'force.' They are modern, uninstructed, rather nebulous Deists."

The professor was right; one of the largest groups of present-day doubters is the multitude who believe in God, but only in a nonpersonal way. They see Him as a great force, the creator of all, in some sense even a personality. But He is grasped as far removed from the dynamic of personal daily life. They are what used to be called Deists. They are found everywhere, but especially on college and high school campuses.

Before we attempt any response to this phenomenon of "neo-Deism," it will help to examine the position of a famous, historical Deist. Understanding him may aid us in comprehending his contemporary counterpart.

Francois Marie Arouet may not be a readily recognizable name unless we mention his nickname: Voltaire—the best known Deist of all time. Many think of Voltaire as an atheist, but he was actually a Deist. Voltaire was born in Paris and died there eighty-three years later. He became the most startling and satirical spokesman for the eighteenth-century deistic spirit, a spirit that seriously challenged historical Christianity.

What is this deistic approach that Voltaire espoused? In *A Handbook of Theological Terms*, Van A. Harvey defines Deism as "the view that regards God as the intelligent creator of an independent and law-abiding world but denies that he providentially guides it or intervenes in any way with its course of destiny."[1] Although embracing a vague belief in God, Deism is for all practical purposes atheistic. God is merely a great, creative force, having no actual involvement in the earthly affairs of life. D. Elton Trueblood explains: "How easy it is to use the word 'God' and mean very little is shown vividly by the history of . . . deistic . . . belief . . . . Though the term is now seldom used, a great deal of what passes for belief today is sheer deism and nothing more and is, therefore, woefully inadequate . . . . Deism may actually be less religious than primitive atheistic Buddhism."[2]

Deism began as an effort to accommodate historic Christianity to "the age of reason." The motivation for the movement was perhaps commendable, but in the struggle Deists became more and more non-Christian as they divorced themselves from biblical Christian teachings, especially those aspects of Christian doctrine that deal with dynamic religious experience. Voltaire's philosophy reached the point where he no longer believed in a God who reveals Himself, let alone acts dramatically in human affairs. G. R. Cragg describes in graphic terms what happened in the minds of Deists like Voltaire:

> [God] was scaled down and domesticated. . . .He was abstract and remote; he was no longer inconvenient because he no longer encountered man with an exacting personal demand. "I believe in God," said Voltaire, "not the God of the mystics and

---

1. Van A. Harvey, *Handbook of Theological Terms* (New York: Macmillan, 1964), p. 66.
2. D. Elton Trueblood, *Philosophy of Religion* (Grand Rapids: Baker, 1977), pp. 260-61.

the theologians, but the God of nature, the great geometrician, the architect of the universe, the prime mover, unalterable, transcendental, everlasting." Such a God stood entirely outside the drama of human history; he could not be connected with anything that happens on this insignificant planet. He built the machine, and set it in motion, but the machine now runs its predetermined course in complete independence of its maker. . . .The God they [Deists] retained inevitably faded into the abstraction of the first cause.[3]

Although many of our contemporary neo-Deists certainly have not worked out a systematic doctrine as the above quotation implies, still there are a host who *practically* live just as if they had. Voltaire's faith and hope was not rooted in a personal God who instructs and inspires us concerning the art of living, let alone identifies with us and dies for us in His Son. He argued that people did not need, nor even wish, God to interfere with the machine He had created and set in motion. Voltaire held that through reason alone one can discover all one needs to know about God, and above all, what everyone needs to know in order to succeed in life. Reason became his personal god. Will Durant states, "Voltaire believed in reason always: 'we can, by speech and pen, make men more enlightened and better.' "[4]

Voltaire wielded his pen with unusual ability. In so doing, he became "for the better part of half a century. . .the most powerful influence in European thought."[5] He possessed one of the most dazzling personalities to leave its mark on recent times. The following description of Voltaire is an ample appetizer to create interest in his views.

Unprepossessing, ugly, vain, flippant, obscene, unscrupulous, even at times dishonest—Voltaire was a man with the faults of his time and place, missing hardly one. And yet this same Voltaire turns out to have been tirelessly kind, considerate, lavish of his energy and his purse, so sedulous in helping friends as in crushing enemies, able to kill with a stroke of his pen and yet disarmed by the first advance of conciliation; so contradictory is man.[6]

3. G. R. Cragg, *The Church and the Age of Reason, 1648-1789* (Baltimore: Penguin, 1970), p. 237.
4. Will Durant, *The Story of Philosophy* (New York: Pocket Books, 1958), p. 247.
5. Cragg, p. 239.
6. Durant, p. 199.

Voltaire achieved fame as a writer and thinker largely because of his indomitable spirit. During his life he overcame imprisonments (in the infamous Bastille), smallpox and other health problems, exile, scandals (eloping with another man's wife with whom he lived for fifteen years before she left him for a younger lover), and the persistent evils of intolerance and prejudice. In his last days, Paris showered with him praise. Even Benjamin Franklin brought his grandson to meet and be "blessed" by Voltaire. During his life he was admired and courted by Frederick the Great, Edward Gibbon, Catherine the Great, and many other notables.

Often quite self-indulgent and belligerent toward others, Voltaire still must be recognized as a warrior against ignorance and prejudice. His greatness — despite his practical atheism—can be seen in the declaration of his war against religious bigotry in the town of Toulouse, France. Catholic persecution of Protestants had become an entrenched way of life. It reached its most degenerate and despicable level with the arrest, torture, and death of a Protestant man who had been falsely accused of murdering his son. Actually, the son had committed suicide. The man's family sought the aid of Voltaire. He courageously responded. In that situation Voltaire adopted what became his motto: *"Erasez l'infame"* (Crush the Infamy). That motto expressed perfectly Voltaire's all-out effort to stamp out prejudice.

In the end "the verdict was reviewed by the king and council and was reversed. . . . Intolerance suffered a mortal blow, and it was fondly assumed that the judicial punishment of religious beliefs had been discredited for ever."[7] This became perhaps Voltaire's greatest hour, a time in which we even see a Christian-like concern for the victims of injustice.

It must be granted that Voltaire had the courage and intelligence to attack bad religion, but he failed to use his outstanding ability to appreciate good religion. G. R. Cragg pinpoints some of his particular weaknesses: "He was a superb critic but a mediocre philosopher . . . he drew heavily (and not always exactly) on the English Deists. . . . From the Deists, Voltaire drew the arguments with which he attacked miracles, prophecy and the authority of Scriptures . . . (and his reasoning) was increasingly obscured by violent antipathies."[8]

7. Cragg, p. 242.
8. Ibid., p. 239.

Still, Voltaire, a man of profound influence, converted many to Deism. And his approach lingers still. Many young people, as well as others, believe in God, but in an impersonal, uninvolved way. They are for justice and reason, but they reject a personal experience of an involved God. They are modern day Deists — modern Voltaires.

AN ANSWER

In answering the deistic spirit, there are but two fundamental questions to pose: First, what is the *end result* of Deism? Second, what are the *means to this end;* that is, what is the system's basic methodology (presuppositions, assumptions, and so on)? In seeking the answers to these two basic queries, the tragic weakness of Deism is uncovered; then the positive claims of Christ can be presented. The answer to the Deist is actually quite brief and straightforward.

THE END RESULT: THE FIRST ISSUE

The Deists' fundamental trust in the omnicompetence of human reason led them to cut away from Christianity anything that related a transcendent God to practical life. They felt all reality had to be discovered and verified by their own human, rational processes.[9] Any form of personal revelational trust was rejected. Consequently, and not surprisingly, their image of God was reduced to that of a vague force or intelligence that had nothing to do with practical, human life on earth. That is the end result. And that is exactly where the problem lies.

That deistic position leaves us with a God who, in the final analysis, is not really God at all. This Highest Being—though He may have created this vast universe and have some sort of personality — in twentieth-century terminology is little more than a cosmological computer creator.

The Deists do not necessarily deny the personality of God; they deny personal involvement of God in the personal affairs of people. Thus His personality does not *really* matter in the dynamics of anyone's personal affairs. God is an "impersonal personality," if there can be such a thing in Deity.

Such a God lacks the highest attribute known to us: involved

9. J. K. S. Reid, *Christian Apologetics* (Grand Rapids: Eerdmans, 1969), p. 140.

personality. But that is hardly tenable, as argued in chapter 2. How could the highest of human concepts, personhood (and that surely implies involvement in other personalities), be denied in the highest reality: a creating God? We, the creation, are persons of involvement ourselves. How could our Creator be less? A creator could hardly create a higher order than himself. It is inconsistent. Trueblood targets this untenable end result of Deism: "There is a fundamental absurdity in supposing that the God in whom he [the Deist] believes is inferior to himself in the *order of being*. If God is a mere 'power,' and not a center of consciousness, then I, the humble creature, am actually superior, in a very important way, to the Creator."[10]

In other words, the deistic creator is inferior to His creation because of His noninvolved personhood. That does not make sense, even the rational sense that Voltaire so relied upon. How can God be God at all if He is not a personal, loving, forgiving, redeeming, involved person?

One wonders if Voltaire did not later in life begin to sense his essential error. It is noticeably ironic to hear him say near the end, "I die adoring God, loving my friends, not hating my enemies, and detesting superstition."[11] How could he possibly *adore* a God who was not an involved Being? For a man characterized as "the most brilliant. . . figure of the Enlightenment,"[12] those dying words are ironically sad.

Voltaire's conclusion reduces his position to an absurdity. *Reductio ad absurdum* may appear too strong a phrase to describe the end result of Deism. But there it is; does it make sense to reduce the definition of God so that He is, in a very fundamental sense, less than us?

THE MEANS TO THE END: THE SECOND ISSUE

In the final analysis, Deism ends in a theology almost totally devoid of God, at least for all practical purposes. How could that happen when Deism began as a movement to reconcile faith to reason, to serve as a friend of religion, not an enemy? The answer is found in the Deists' methodology.

Deists like Voltaire presuppose that religion, to be viable in

---

10. Trueblood, p. 265.
11. Durant, p. 250.
12. Eugene Weber, *The Western Tradition* (Boston: D. C. Heath, 1965), p. 490.

the modern world, must be based primarily on rational reason. Voltaire became convinced that since the age of reason had arrived, no one with a sensible approach to life would accept anything that was not purely rational. Now it is obvious that Christian truth focuses essentially on the initiative of God in revealing Himself through creation, the Israelites, and ultimately Jesus Christ. Revelation is above rationalism in biblical Christianity.

That does not mean Christian truth is *anti*-rational. It is merely *beyond* human rationalism in its revelational aspects. If there is no conflict between reason and revelation, then no problem exists. But if there is a conflict, for example, like the bodily resurrection of Jesus Christ, then biblical Christians must opt for revelation. After all, God, if He be ultimate, is above *all* human categories, including human rationalism. Thus it is vital for God to *reveal* Himself. That automatically puts revelation *above* human reason in discovering God's truth. That is why Christians opt for revelation rather than reason if a conflict between the two occurs. And that is sensible and coherent. (That is what philosopher Francis Schaeffer calls a "presuppositional apologetic.")

Deists prefer to think of man as the discoverer of God rather than God the Revealer-Redeemer for man. In short, Deists are convinced that they possess the ability to discover God without any revelation from God. In fact they often have disdain for scriptural revelation, choosing to condemn prophecy and miracles as being nothing but superstition. Is that wise? Is that a coherent approach?

Many serious problems arise with the deistic approach. For example, is it reasonable to believe that mortal humans can discover the immortal God without divine revelation? Is it reasonable for finite creatures to be unconcerned about receiving assistance from the infinite God? Is it reasonable for sinful people to think they can rationally describe a righteous and holy God? The key question is: How can limited human beings know an unlimited God unless He reveals Himself? Revelation is mandatory. Moreover, a pressing practical question confronts the modern Deist who is following in the footsteps of Voltaire: While it is obvious that Voltaire fought against prejudice in others, did he not overlook his own prejudice concerning the whole realm of revelation? His purely rational presupposition forced him to a closed position on revelation; that is an epistemological prejudice—Voltaire's methodology is flawed from the start. Such a methodology is bound to end in faulty conclusions.

The previous questions should encourage the open-minded Deist to reexamine his basic presuppositions, methodology, and biases that tend automatically to rule out the role of God's personal revelation. If the Deist can open himself to the possibility of revelation from the God he says he believes in, the whole of Christianity then opens up to him.

CONCLUSION

The weakness of *pure* rationalism to describe God is evident. That case should now have been well made. But can a thoroughly convincing case be made for the validity of revelation? That is the crux of the matter. How can believers in Jesus Christ present the principle of revelational truth so as to help the doubter? To elucidate that vital, central agrument we now turn to the final chapter on the humanist skeptic.

10

The Humanist Skeptic

No deity will save us: we must save ourselves.

— *Humanist Manifesto I and II*

What is back of all the doubt and skepticism we have been considering in the previous chapters? Seen from the spiritual perspective, it is the old battle of satanic deception. Coupled with human sin, it blinds the minds of those who do not believe (2 Corinthians 4:3). From the *human* perspective it is just that: *humanism*. Viewed from a temporal vantage point, humanism of some sort, and to some degree, is the ultimate source of disbelief.

The spirit of humanism has been with us for eons. It started in the Garden of Eden when Adam and Eve were expelled, and it has run through the course of history to the contemporary moment. For many millennia it was more or less a spirit, or attitude, or approach to life. In recent days, however, it has been formalized into a widespread, systematized philosophy. It has been integrated into ethics, epistemology, religious concepts, and so on. No aspect of thought has been ignored by the humanists.

It must be acknowledged that humanists are asking the right question: How can life be filled with meaning? That is a commendable, vital query. It should be asked by all. However, it is the answer the humanist comes up with that presents the problem.

In the final analysis, humanism is the spirit that lies behind Freud, Camus, the Huxleys, Nietzsche, Darrow, Russell, Altizer, Voltaire, and virtually every other brand of skepticism and doubt. To a greater or lesser degree, they each attempt to answer the basic questions of life without God and then try to live as if God were not vital to finding life's meaning. That is the root of virtually all skeptical problems. We believers *must* recognize the force of this humanistic spirit and approach. It is the basic challenge of our day.

MODERN HUMANISM

More than a few college professors teach that humanism is the religion of today and surely tomorrow. They contend that Christianity is outdated and outdone. Several award-winning scientists agree. They believe we must all embrace humanism because it is the only way to save the world. They do have high motives; that must be granted. And the fact that they have been heard and heeded by many is obvious. Sociological data tells us that the primary principles of humanism are affecting our society more than any other value system or philosophy. This presents a real problem. Christians are called to react, but must be careful not to overreact. We must not get so disturbed that we respond to the challenge in an un-Christian manner or careless way. On the other hand, we cannot afford to underreact. We need to study carefully this professed enemy of Christianity.

Who are some of the leading personalities in the movement? The booklet entitled *Humanist Manifestos I and II* lists some of those who have demonstrated their support for humanism by signing the Manifesto. Self-proclaimed humanists include Andrei Sakharov, B. F. Skinner, Corliss Lamont, Betty Friedan, Sir Julian Huxley, Sidney Hook, Jacques Monod, Gunnar Myrdal, and nearly three hundred other people who are labeled as "distinguished leaders of thought and action." Other prominent people who identify themselves as humanists are politicians, writers, professors, teachers, scientists, plus a large number of Unitarian ministers.

What is humanism as advocated by these influential people? On page three of *Humanist Manifestos I and II* we read,

> Humanism is a philosophical, religious, and moral point of view as old as human civilization itself. . . . In 1933 a group of thirty-four liberal humanists in the United States. . . drafted

Humanist Manifesto I, which for its time was a radical document. It. . . rejected orthodox and dogmatic positions. . . it did not go far enough. . . [therefore], forty years later *Humanist Manifesto II* was drafted.[1]

What do the subscribers to this booklet believe about religion? The *Manifesto* states, "Traditional religions. . . inhibit humans from helping themselves or experiencing their full potentialities. . . . No deity will save us; we must save ourselves. . . . Promises of immortal salvation or fear of eternal damnation are both illusory and harmful. . . . Traditional religions. . . are obstacles to human progress."[2]

Corliss Lamont, one of the speakers for humanism, writes that the New Testament is totally alien to the humanist viewpoint. He and others reject the whole idea of people being sinners with a selfish nature. What do these humanists say concerning morality? They declare, "We reject all religions. . . or moral codes that denigrate the individual, suppress freedom. . . . In the area of sexuality we believe that intolerant attitudes, often cultivated by orthodox religions and puritanical cultures, unduly repress sexual conduct. . . a civilized society should be a tolerant one."[3]

Dr. Mary Calderone, 1974 Humanist of the Year, states that teenagers should experiment with sex and that extramarital sex may be good for people. She declares, "An extramarital affair that's really solid might have very good results."[4] Of course, not all humanists ascribe to that level of sexual morality.

To state it simply, humanism centers primarily on humanity, while Christianity is focused first on God and then on mankind. The societies of Greece and Rome were often quite human-centered, despite their pagan religions; but, as Christianity took root, Western societies began to give attention to God and how our relationship with God influences our relationship with each other. But since the Renaissance, the humanistic approach has experienced a significant rebirth and is now moving forward in full stride.

Karl Marx probably expressed the central concept of humanism best when he argued, "The root of mankind is man

---

1. *Humanist Manifestos I and II* (Buffalo, N.Y.: Prometheus Books, 1973), p. 3.
2. Ibid., pp. 16-17.
3. Ibid., p. 18.
4. Tim LaHaye, *The Battle for the Mind* (Old Tappan, N.J.: Revell, 1980), p. 66.

not God." Doctrinaire humanists reject belief in God as the core of life. They feel the cure of humanity's ills rests in humanity itself, not God. Therefore, they seem to want to rewrite many of God's laws, recreate persons through education, training, genetic engineering, and behavioral conditioning, and thus alter God's world by building a humanistic heaven on earth. What can we say to the doubter who is plagued with this skeptical attitude?

The defense that follows is broadened to include answers for all types of humanism, not just the systematized and doctrinaire aspects of the movement. It is intended to help all the varieties of skepticism presented in the previous chapters.

AN ANSWER

First we need to understand how far reaching the philosophy has spread. To hear Nobel Prize winner Francis Crick advocate that an elite group of scientific thinkers should determine who is to be born and who is to die is indeed disturbing. He believes that "some group of people should decide that some people should have more children and some should have fewer. . . . You have to decide who is to be born."[5]

We should be concerned when we realize that the 1975 Humanist of the Year and head of the Women's Activist group, Betty Friedan, holds that our traditional values and life-styles need to be wiped out. It is disquieting to realize that Harvard professor B. F. Skinner teaches that we are nothing but products of genetics and environment and therefore he, and others like him, should be permitted to use behavioral conditioning to improve humanity at the expense of our freedom, which he believes is not real anyway. Skinner labels those who disagree with him as neurotic and psychotic.[6] And when Mary Calderone and others endorse and encourage the new morality based on teenage sexual experimentation, living together, extramarital affairs, and abortion on demand, we must respond.

Often Christians are tempted to write such people off as extremists whose concepts will never find a following. But we must recognize they are in positions of authority and

5. Francis A. Schaeffer, *Back to Freedom and Dignity* (Downers Grove, Ill.: InterVarsity, 1974), p. 22.
6. Ibid., p. 45.

influence. For example, Crick is one of the leading men in the field of genetics. Skinner is an outstanding psychologist. Friedan is a leading feminist. Their attitude has permeated society more than we may ever realize. One humanist, Rousseau, had a tremendous influence on the instigation and outcome of the French Revolution.

Once we gauge the seriousness of the challenge, the next step is to identify the major difference between Christianity and the general humanistic attitude. If we can demonstrate the vast superiority of Christianity as a philosophy and life-style, we will be on the way toward responding to the skeptic. Jesus said, "You will know them by their fruits" (Matthew 7:16).

Humanists say that their creed is as old as human civilization itself. That is true. An ancient form of humanism, remarkably similar to modern versions, is found in Genesis 11: The Tower of Babel story. Here a people had lost their relationship with God. So they decided to create their own human-centered religion and prove their greatness by building a tower that would reach high into the Mid-East sky. It would be a super tower built by super people and thus solidify and unify their society. As one biblical scholar points out: They had lost their religion based on God, but realized they needed something to keep them united; therefore, they created their own religion which would be symbolized by the Tower of Babel.

Their basic philosophy held that people could make it without God, without thinking about sin, without obeying a definite revealed and authoritative code of morality. But it all collapsed. The Tower of Babel became the symbol not of unity but of division and chaos. Their "new world" never came off. Humanism ultimately divides. You simply cannot build a viable society on mere humanistic foundations. This is God's world. Only God can lay a lasting base for successful social structures. All history testifies to that fact. The fruit of humanism is chaos.

That same truth can be seen in the contemporary results of the humanistic-communistic dream of comradeship: the Iron and Bamboo Curtains. Helmut Thielicke, German theologian and pastor writes,

> Suppose I have a business partner who believes in nothing, for whom there is no authority whatsoever, to say nothing of the commandments of God, a man in whom I cannot find any-

thing that looks like inner sanction. I would be on guard against such a man. I could distrust him. Perhaps I could be afraid of him. . . if he is no longer subject to God, then he is under the domination of his instincts, his opportunism, his will to power.[7]

Further, how can humanists overlook the gross inhumanity in human history without God? The tragedy and irony of the humanistic spirit is that it becomes a religion created by humans, for humans, and under the direction of humans, yet it is so often insensitive to individual persons. Hard core humanists say that individual persons are nothing but chemical machines, the accidental result of evolution. Consequently, the individual is expendable—if he or she is too old, too stupid, or too troublesome. Not all degenerate to that level, of course, but humanism at least leans in that direction. Unless men and women are conscious of being made in God's image, the essential dignity of being human can well be lost. That is a fruit of the humanist approach—if not initially, it will be eventually.

Doctrinaire humanists tend to believe that the end justifies the means. A purely secular, humanistic approach often seems to say that individuals really do not matter most. As an illustration, there is an old Jewish legend about the builders of the Tower of Babel. They were not disturbed when construction workers were killed. What upset them was to see a brick broken. They were preoccupied with the Tower, not the individual workman building it. Although most educated humanists are certainly not so calloused nor would go to such extremes, when one dismisses the restraining hand of a loving, caring, personal God in human affairs, inhumanity to man can soon follow—and often does. Only where the gospel has permeated society does one find a high value placed on individual lives. History clearly attests to that.

The unpleasant surprise for the present-day Tower of Babel builders is the fact that the end result is not at all as expected. For example, has humanism given Sweden—where humanism virtually reigns supreme—a more full and meaningful life? True, people's material needs are taken care of, and that is important and good. But are the people better off morally with humanism rather than Christianity? Are they

7. Helmut Theilicke, *How the World Began* (Philadelphia: Fortress, 1974), p. 281.

happier? Does life have more reality? A study of young people reveals that many are not interested in getting married, having children, and doing well in a job. Hardly any are happy. A study of old people is even more depressing. Most are miserable, while many are trying to decide whether or not to commit suicide, which is legal in Sweden—and the suicide rate is appalling.

But the humanists still continue in building their Tower. Granted, all humanists do not plunge into amoralism, but many do. Their basic philosophy tends to promote it. That, too, is one of their fruits. When we sow to the wind, we reap the whirlwind (Hosea 8:7).

But there is still a big hurdle in commending Christianity to the humanist. Although the skeptic may be to some degree attracted by what Christianity appears to offer, he may have difficulty believing that a revelational faith can be completely true and reliable and thus able to deliver on its claims. It finally reduces itself to this: Can one believe that the Bible reveals God's truth and is thus a true testimony to God, reality, and a genuine meaningful life?

Can one build life on the Scriptures? Can a person really trust the Bible—a book that seems so strange, so old, and so confusing to so many—as God's truth revealed? Can we commend the Bible to the humanistic doubter? These are the questions.

The relationship between revelation and the Bible is a major study in itself. There is in some sense a difference between God personally addressing a person in revelation and the objective book called the Bible. Yet there is an intrinsic connection; the Bible does reveal God's truth. The Scriptures will do the work as the "sharp, two-edged sword" of the Spirit. God will address people through the means of the Scriptures.

Our goal should be to arouse curiosity in the mind of the doubting, humanist skeptic so that the Bible will be opened, read, and studied with an open mind. Then, we must pray that the Spirit of God will speak to the reader and reveal Jesus Christ. As the doubter reads, it may well be that the revelation of God will break in on him. In helping the skeptic acquire an interest in God's Word, we can point out the following realities. There are five miracles of revelation the Word of God presents. These should aid the doubter in arousing interest and acceptance of the Bible.

The first miracle of revelation (the term "miracle" is used here and following not in a strict sense; but, rather, to profile the Bible as God's holy, inspired, authoritative Word) is recorded in the very first chapter of Genesis: "In the beginning God created. . . ." Even the skeptical Voltaire accepted the fact that God had created the heavens. Albert Einstein and a host of other scientific thinkers granted this. Einstein said that when the scientists and cosmologists finally arrive at the top of the mountain they will find that the theologians have been there for years.

Many scientists, theologians, and a host of common people know there has to be some sort of first cause. For God to be the First Cause really provides the most sensible *ultimate* cosmology. Whether we accept the idea of the "Big Bang," constant creation, or whatever cosmological theory we find attractive, there still remains the necessity for a First Cause back of it all.

Thus it seems clear that the very fabric of the universe itself becomes a revelation reminding us that this "time-space capsule," to use Einstein's terminology, points to a creating first cause God. And where can we discover a reasonable account of the activity of this First Cause? Nowhere is there an account comparable to that found in the Bible. As Harold O. J. Brown observes, "Scientists in growing numbers are once again facing the question of First Cause and are postulating—some even confessing—that the First Cause is the personal God of Scripture."[8]

Brown cites Benedictine monk and physicist Stanley L. Jaki's work when he explains how "present reality points with increasing clarity to an instantaneous origin in time:. . .it does describe a *creation*, not an eternally existing universe, and certainly not a fortuitous 'happening.' "[9] The Scripture stands on its own as a record of creation, presenting the most coherent cosmology to be found.

The second miracle of revelation is mentioned in Genesis 17:7-8. In this passage, the Bible designates the descendants of Abraham as the chosen people of God. Historical evidence, ancient and modern, points to the validity of the biblical claim. Abraham's descendants are surely the miracle people

---

8. Harold O. J. Brown, "Current Religious Thought," *Christianity Today* (12 December 1980), p. 76.
9. Brown, p. 76.

of history. The Jewish people not only survived the enslavement in Egypt, they actually thrived in that cruel context (Exodus 1:12). Despite indescribable oppression, the Jews proved to be indestructible. They escaped slavery, struggled through the wilderness, made it to a prosperous and fruitful land, conquered that land, and then established a small but vibrant nation that held its ground against incredible odds and innumerable enemies. Furthermore, although the Jews later became "a people without a country" for two thousand years, they kept their national identity and reclaimed their land in 1948. Since then they have protected and expanded their territory when attacked by enemies outnumbering them a hundred to one.

Furthermore, the Jewish people have made a tremendous impact in our world, far out of proportion to their small numbers. Think of the great minds that the Jews have produced, in the twentieth century alone—for example, Albert Einstein. There are Jews in all fields whose stature can scarcely be measured. God's providence is surely present in all their struggles.

Moreover, the Jewish experience points to the fact that there is purpose and an end in history. Evidence demonstrates that God is involved in human history and that all of creation moves toward a goal. This argument is often termed the teleological proof for God. And where do we learn about the roots and purpose of all these movements? In the Bible. It presents these revealed realities in a way no other source can.

A third miracle of revelation is summarized in John 1:14, "And the Word became flesh, and dwelt among us, and we beheld His glory, glory as of the only begotten from the Father, full of grace and truth." The Bible says God has finally and fully revealed Himself in His own Son. Some of these ideas were presented earlier, but they bear more evidence here. William Barclay wrote about Jesus Christ, the miracle of miracles, "The evidence of [Jesus'] miracles is good and well nigh unanswerable; but the best evidence of all is *Jesus Himself*."[10] His miraculous life should be evidence enough. Jesus' Sermon on the Mount is extraordinary, but what is miraculous is the fact that He practiced what He preached—perfectly, undeniably. No one else has.

10. William Barclay, *And He Had Compassion* (Valley Forge, Pa.: Judson, 1977), p. 27.

Rousseau, a humanist, noting that Plato dreamed about a perfect man, declared that only Jesus lived up to and personified that dream. Philosopher John Stuart Mill stated that no one could have invented or imagined a person as good as Jesus. Although both Ralph Waldo Emerson and David Strauss had problems believing in miraculous revelation, they conceded that Jesus was morally perfect, a miracle in and of itself. The only logical conclusion is that Jesus is the personal and convincing revelation that God exists and is Himself the way to God.

Now where do we learn of the miraculous life, death, and resurrection of Jesus the Christ? In the Bible. That is the *only* place we can come to grips with the revelation of God in Christ. Thus the Scriptures produce revelational truth like none other.

Growing out of that fact is the fourth miracle of revelation. It is described in Paul's letter to the Corinthians:

> Now I make known to you, brethren, the gospel which I preached to you, which also you received, in which also you stand by which also you are saved, if you hold fast the word which I preached to you, unless you believed in vain. For I delivered to you as of first importance what I also received, that Christ died for our sins according to the Scriptures, and that He was buried, and that He was raised on the third day according to the Scriptures, and that He appeared to Cephas [Peter], then to the twelve. After that He appeared to more than five hundred brethren at one time, most of whom remain until now, but some have fallen asleep; then He appeared to James, then to all the apostles; and last of all, as it were to one untimely born, He appeared to me also . . . . And if Christ has not been raised, then our preaching is vain, your faith also is vain. (1 Corinthians 15:1-8, 14)

When Jesus was crucified, it looked as if all was lost. But when the Lord was resurrected three days later the Christian faith was gloriously established. Christianity is first and foremost a resurrection faith. What a miracle of revelation that divine act is! Of course, the resurrection is a revelational truth to be grasped by faith. Yet at the same time, there are some purely empirical, rational, historical evidences that point to the resurrection. Granted, they may not rationally *prove* the resurrection. They are only evidences, but they are there and must be reckoned with.

The critics of Christianity have done their best to give rational reasons to disprove the resurrection. But the empirical evidence is too much to dismiss summarily. For example, Dr. Simon Greenleaf, professor of law at Harvard University, recognized by the Chief Justice of the Supreme Court to be the greatest authority on legal evidence who has ever lived, decided to examine the evidence relating to the resurrection. Following a detailed study, he concluded that in any unbiased courtroom in the world the evidence would fully establish the fact that Jesus was resurrected from the dead. Belief in the resurrection is supported by some hard, empirical facts:

> The empty tomb
> The five hundred people who saw the resurrected Christ
> The radically-changed lives of the disciples
> The disciples' willingness to die for their faith
> The birth and growth of the church

There is simply no fully satisfying, truly adequate explanation for these known facts except the resurrection. Of course, other explanations for the evidences can be given, if one is of a mind to do so, but as one historian admitted, "Although I am not a Christian I cannot deny the evidence for the resurrection." And again, we learn of the glorious fact of the resurrection of Jesus Christ through the Bible. How difficult it is to avoid the conclusion that the Word of God deals with revelational reality.

The fifth miracle of revelation concerns the Bible itself. Many of the attacks on historic Christianity rest on the assumption that the Bible is no more than a good book. The skeptic usually grants that the Bible is an excellent book on ethics, morals, and so on, but he refuses to accept it as an authoritative Word from God. The argument is that the Scriptures are not reliable when it comes to prophecy, miracles, and the supernatural revelation of God's truth. Some even deny its historicity, but that attack has become less common.

Now if the Bible is successfully refuted as presenting God's revealed truth, we Christians are in trouble. But look at the evidence that helps substantiate our position. First, there is the fact that the Scriptures have survived thousands of years of intense criticism. No book has been studied and attacked so vigorously and yet survived unscathed and is still believed by intelligent millions. Further, the Bible's prophecies have, up to this point in time, come true. Not only that, the historical accuracy of the Bible has been proven over and over. The more the archaeologists dig, the more evidence they find to substantiate the Bible.

A classic example is in the case of Pontius Pilate. For years no archaeological evidence was found to substantiate the Bible's claims about this person. Thus, some declared the Bible was historically inaccurate. A few years ago a stone was unearthed at Caesarea with Pilate's name on it. Similar situations have been multiplied over and again.

Then there is the fact that the Bible presents an honest picture of people as well as the best picture of God, creation, and so on. The Scriptures "tell it like it is"; the Bible whitewashes nothing. It has the ring of truth. The Bible answers the basic, fundamental questions of life. Perhaps above all, it speaks dynamically to the very heart of those who will read its pages openly and honestly. These and many other evidences of the uniqueness of the Bible demand attention. The most sensible answer is that the Bible is God's authoritative truth. How does one really account for it otherwise?

Thus the Christian contends that the Bible is a supernaturally given Word. But the greatest and final argument of the Bible's validity rests in the fact that God Himself speaks through its pages, and lives are miraculously changed. The Holy Spirit uses it to inspire faith and commitment towards God. God has spoken countless times through the Bible, and millions of people have been healed, inspired, changed, and reborn. That is an undeniable evidential fact. To attempt to deny it is to close one's eyes to reality.

Furthermore, believers have come to see that *anyone* who reads the Bible prayerfully, carefully, sincerely, and with a willingness to yield one's life to God, will be confronted by the living God Himself.

To illustrate this prime argument, J. Edwin Orr tells the story of his encounter with a young lady who had just lost her husband in a plane crash. Her father had died five months before, and her mother was also deceased. All she had was her husband, and now he was gone. She cried uncontrollably as Edwin Orr tried unsuccessfully to comfort her. Then he began to read the twenty-third Psalm, and suddenly a strange calm came over the young widow. Peace flooded her very soul. Orr asks the question, "Why did I not read a line from Omar Khayyam or William Shakespeare?" He answered, "I know the *transforming power of Scripture!*"

Another well-known story that illuminates the power of God's Word revolves around the experience of Sergeant DeShazer, a bombardier who flew on the famous Doolittle raid on Tokyo during World War II. His plane ran out of fuel, and he and the rest of the crew were forced to parachute into Japanese territory. They were captured, imprisoned, and severely mistreated by their captors. They were treated like animals, and life became almost unbearable. Then the prisoners began passing around a Bible. DeShazer's turn came, and as he read it for a few days, it radically changed his life. One day, as the guards were beating him, he remembered the words of Jesus that he had just read: "Love your enemies." A strange peace came over him. His remarkable attitude so impressed the guards that they stopped beating him and never touched him again.

After the war DeShazer became a missionary and returned to Japan where he met some of his old prison guards. They were amazed at his ability to love them. They began studying the Bible and were soon converted. Mitsuo Fuchida, the Japanese officer who led the air attack on Pearl Harbor, read about DeShazer's work and was so inspired that he contacted Christian missionaries, began reading the Bible, and experienced conversion to Christ. God does confront people in and through the Word.

These stories can be repeated again and again. Through the ages, when people have begun reading and applying the simple gospel of the Bible, great transformations have occurred. History literally abounds with such experiences in a way that no other religion chronicles. With the Bible in her hand and in her heart, Florence Nightingale achieved marvelous results. She revolutionized hospital care and inaugurated the nursing profession. John Howard, with the Bible in his heart and mind, quite miraculously changed a prison system that was like a hell on earth. By the Word of God, Dorothea Dix succeeded in getting mentally ill patients out of dungeons and into hospitals. Robert Raikes, armed with the Bible, courageously pioneered a program of caring for street urchins who were roaming the lanes and alleys of England. William Wilberforce led the fight to outlaw slavery on the basis of the Bible. Through the power of the Word, Theodore

Weld moved the abolition movement forward in America. No other book has done what the Bible has. It is just a fact of history.

But if the Bible is a "Miracle Book," why do so many people have difficulty getting into it and seeing changes take place in their lives? That is a genuine problem for many doubters. What can help solve this quandary?

There are at least three reasons for difficulty with the Bible. First, some are threatened by the Bible. For instance, the humanistic libertine who wants to justify in his own mind his sin and selfishness knows that the Bible, with its ethical ideals, is his archenemy. For people who want no more than to do "their own thing," the Bible with its code of morality is a clear and unmistakable foe. Thus, they willingly turn away. As Jesus said, they "loved the darkness rather than the light; for their deeds were evil" (John 3:19). That is the root of much skepticism.

Second, some people find the Bible difficult to understand because they never seriously study it. We can sympathize, at least to a degree, with such people; the Bible is not an easy book to understand. However, just because the Bible is at times more difficult to read than a popular novel, that is certainly no reason to reject it. It takes God's help to understand His Word, but anyone who wishes to know God's truth in the Bible will surely have that help. And the reward more than repays the effort. Bible study is surely worth it all. Life can be found there. If the humanist doubter will read, God will speak. That leads to the third reason, which is akin to the first.

Some people refuse to believe in the Bible because they refuse to humble themselves enough to read the Bible with a view to obeying it. We are not only to read the Bible, but we are also called to heed it. This, in a sense, is really the crux of the matter. One must permit the Holy Spirit to speak through the revealed Word and give grace to obey it. We have discovered that almost every critic of the Bible tends to lack humility and is simply rebellious against God's will. They want to master the Bible rather than let the Bible master them.

The point is, humanists of all persuasions can find the reality of God in Christ *if they will.* That is the issue: if they will. God is found by those who seek Him with all their hearts. To the humble and submissive, He makes His revelation known. The Word of God will speak for itself.

CONCLUSION

Christ and the biblical gospel make real sense. It is not a blind leap into the dark. The person willing to acknowledge his or her sin and need of Jesus Christ—that is, honestly face his own reality—will always find Him. The Scriptures are powerful indeed and reveal God's truth. Thus the Bible stands. It declares truth. Of course no one is ever brought to Christ by mere argument alone. Yet, we are to "always [be] ready to make a defense to everyone who asks you to give an account for the hope that is in you" (1 Peter 3:15).

God's truth will prevail and speak to the heart—even the skeptical heart. Humbly and graciously, but with genuine confidence, share the full gospel with all. There are a multitude of helps today in presenting the message of Jesus Christ. Much published material in this area is available—use it. But above all, present Jesus Christ Himself, in word and deed and life.

Epilogue
Responding to a Skeptic: Resources and Power

This final, devotional word will form an epilogue to the appeal for responding to the skeptical doubter. It centers on the principles of discipleship. Perhaps it seems a bit out of place to end a book on witnessing by discussing the essence of a dynamic Christian life-style. But it is not out of place at all. As a matter of fact, it is vital; for what we *are* usually speaks more loudly than what we *say*. Our lives must undergird our witness if it is to be effective at all. There really are resources for successful witnessing. Power is available upon which any believer can draw — power that will enable him to make a significant impact for Christ and His gospel. In the final analysis, only the moving of the Holy Spirit can remove the scales from the unbeliever's eyes. Only the Spirit of God can truly confront the unbeliever with the living Christ. And He works through witnesses whom He can use with power. We must become *powerful* witnesses, using all the resources God grants us.

THE POWER OF A HOLY LIFE

When one's service and sharing are finally summed up, that which makes the most lasting impression is a Christlike, holy life. It has been often said, "A holy life is an awful weapon in God's hand." As a young minister, I once had the opportunity of serving as an associate pastor to a true man of

God — and that term is not used lightly. This man was not the pastor of a large, influential church. He was not an outstanding or eloquent preacher. His intellectual achievements were not extraordinary. Yet his ministry was felt over a large area. Many came to faith in Christ through his witness. Why? The thing that gave him such influence for Christ was the simple godliness of his life. And though he passed on some years ago, the man's impact still remains.

A number of things are implied by his story. In the first place, the image of the effective witness is extremely relevant to the power of his witness. As Gavin Reid has pointed out, "Image communication can have an important *supporting* role to play."[1] Paul recognized that it is essential to be able to say of one's self, "Brethren, join in following my example, and observe those who walk according to the pattern you have in us" (Philippians 3:17). When one can honestly and humbly make such a statement, his life will prove effective in sharing the gospel with the skeptic.

Second, one's native ability is not necessarily the determining factor in an effective witness. Of course, God uses the talents and gifts we have, but only as one's life truly reflects Jesus Christ will God make that life useful in personal evangelism. Therefore, it is vital for all who aspire to winning people to Christ to learn the principles of godly living. The principles of a holy life are few and elemental. The basic concept can be summarized as simply knowing God in the experiential fellowship of Jesus Christ. As John put it in his first epistle,

> What we have seen and heard we proclaim to you also, that you also may have fellowship with us; and indeed our fellowship is with the Father, and with His Son Jesus Christ. And these things we write, so that our joy may be made complete. And this is the message we have heard from Him and announce to you, that God is light, and in Him there is no darkness at all. . . . If we walk in the light as He Himself is in the light, we have fellowship with one another, and the blood of Jesus His Son cleanses us from all sin. (1 John 1:3-5, 7)

That passage makes clear that daily fellowship with Christ — walking in the light as He is in the light — is the essence of

---

1. Gavin Reid, *The Gagging of God* (London: Hodder and Stoughton, 1969), p. 57.

living a powerful, effective, holy life.

Several important principles emerge from the possibility of knowing God in the sense of walking daily in His presence. First, John views fellowship with God as a *marvel*, marvelous because of the fact that "God is light" (v. 5). The metaphor concerning the character of God as "light" is used in several places in the New Testament. This concept of light refers to God's holiness, and from various New Testament passages in which this picture is drawn we can grasp something of the marvel of what it means to walk with the God of holy light. "God is light," said John, "and in Him there is no darkness at all." In other words, God is completely and unequivocally morally perfect. His righteousness is infinite and ultimate. He is *absolute holiness.* God is light — complete light — and in Him is no darkness at all.

What a picture of God! No doubt, a new appreciation of the holiness, sovereignty, and majesty of the God of light is needed. A fresh vision of the glory of God like Ezekiel received is a pressing need. When the prophet saw God for who He actually is, he fell on his face in the dust (Ezekiel 1:28). We must never forget that God is light and His holiness is utterly unapproachable by sinful people in the flesh. Though He is intimately concerned for us all, He is absolutely holy.

That is the nature of the God who invites us to come and walk in fellowship with Himself. What a marvel! What a way to live! Not only is such a life-style quite wonderful, unless we do learn to walk with God in the light, we will probably witness little to the skeptic — or to anyone else for that matter. Christ must be real to us before we will be *motivated* to make Him real to others.

Let it be made clear we are not talking about an unreal, Middle Ages style of mysticism. Rather, we are speaking of the biblical idea conveyed by the Greek word *koinonia:* fellowship with God and one another, permeated by the Holy Spirit's presence.

Yet, when we speak of walking in the light, a problem is precipitated. God is light; that we know, but so often we walk in darkness, the very antithesis of light. Christians hardly need to be reminded that we are often found walking in sins's darkness (1 John 1:8, 10). And light and darkness do not mix. Yet, in spite of it all, we can actually walk with God Almighty in the light. How can it be?

FELLOWSHIP THROUGH CONFESSION

Fellowship with God is a glorious possibility. But, foundational to the pragmatics of the experience is the realization that true fellowship with a holy God begins in dealing with our sins. John tells us,

> If we say that we have fellowship with Him and yet walk in the darkness, we lie and do not practice the truth; but if we walk in the light as He Himself is in the light, we have fellowship with one another, and the blood of Jesus His Son cleanses us from all sin. If we say that we have no sin, we are deceiving ourselves, and the truth is not in us. *If we confess our sins,* He is faithful and righteous to forgive us our sins and to cleanse us from all unrighteousness. (1 John 1:6-9, italics added)

The ultimate enemy that destroys our fellowship, our walk with God, is our personal sin.

How are we to deal with the problem of our personal sin? The fundamental principle is found in 1 John 1:7: "If we walk in the light as He Himself is in the light, we have fellowship with one another, and the blood of Jesus His Son cleanses us from all sin." The key phrase in the verse is the final statement where John says the blood of Jesus, God's Son, *continually* cleanses Christians from all sin. That is the force of the verbal tense John uses. This simply means that if we are to walk in the light we must constantly be cleansed by the power of Christ's forgiveness. In that way alone can we abide in the light. The darkness of our lives must be constantly dispelled (cleansed) by the blood of Christ. That alone effects a constant walk in fellowship with God. That is a basic principle of the holy life. But *how* is the believer to deal with his or her sins in order that the blood of Christ may actually be efficacious in cleansing, thus keeping one in fellowship with the holy God?

Perhaps it would be helpful to recount a personal experience here. A noted missionary spoke in our church one time. In the course of her address she urged us to write what she called one's personal sin account. She instructed everyone to take a piece of paper and on the left-hand column write down several numbers. Then in the quiet of a secret place before God, to pray that the Holy Spirit would reveal every single thing in one's life that was displeasing to Him, that had grieved Him, and that had marred fellowship with

Him, and what had not been brought before His presence individually.

As a Christian, I wanted to be led into all that God had, so I took the missionary seriously. I made out my personal "sin account." Much to my humbling, the Spirit of God brought unconfessed things to my mind that I had committed months, even years ago. The Holy Spirit thoroughly searched me out. I wrote them down. Then, one by one, I brought them back before God and confessed them by acknowledging, with the convicting Holy Spirit, that those things were actually sins of which I was guilty. And when I confessed and forsook them, that is, stood against them as God does, how precious the blood of Christ became. Simply put, the principle is, our sins must be confessed one by one — whether we write them, verbalize them, or whatever. We must be honest with ourselves and God.

Now confession is not to be a time of morbid, neurotic introspection such as some seem to enjoy. That is not healthy and must never be permitted. It is simply an honest evaluation before God. Thus it brings a great release, not depression. Actually, it is a most liberating experience. A new fellowship with God can be found.

Moreover, some of our sins may manifest themselves in relation to others as well as to God. In such cases, to merely confess our sins to God alone is insufficient. To be sure, we should confess them to God. But Jesus also stated in the Sermon on the Mount that if we have sinned against another and at the same time "are presenting your offering at the altar, and there remember that your brother has something against you, leave your offering there before the altar, and go your way; first be reconciled to your brother, and then come and present your offering" (Matthew 5:23-24). We cannot avoid the simple truth presented here; if we sin against another person and our fellowship with him is thus marred, restitution must be made to that person or persons as well as to God. In the light of Jesus' statement, if we fail to acknowledge sins and thus lose fellowship with other persons, then we cannot really expect deep fellowship with God *or one another.*

All of this is to be seen in the most positive light. For when it is maturely and scripturally approached, it is found to be a healing experience. When we open up to God and others, it strips off the facade we tend to hide behind, and thus we become "real" persons.

As we honestly confess our sins, we then claim the promise that God is "faithful and righteous to forgive us our sins and to cleanse us from all unrighteousness" (1 John 1:9). Being forgiven implies a debt remitted or sin dropped; the cleansing implies a stain bleached out. God not only forgives us, He also cleanses us from the stain and thus liberates us to walk in the light as He is in the light. That is real fellowship with Christ and the essence of Christian community. Of course, it goes without saying that when we confess our sins in God's manner as outlined from 1 John, we are genuinely repentant and yielded to God's will for our lives in every detail. There is no forgiveness without true surrender to Christ's leadership in our lives and true repentance when we sin. That is how a holy life begins and is maintained.

VICTORY OVER TEMPTATION

All that has been presented concerning sin and confession should not leave the impression that in Christ there is no victory over daily temptations and that our experience of God is nothing more than temptation, sin, confession, forgiveness, *ad infinitum.* That would hardly be a true holy life, let alone a joyous one (1 John 1:4). The Scriptures are quite clear that God gives power over temptation as one walks in fellowship with Him: "Thanks be to God, who always leads us in His triumph" (2 Corinthians 2:14); "the law of the Spirit of life in Christ Jesus has set you free from the law of sin and of death" (Romans 8:2); "in all these things we overwhelmingly conquer through Him who loved us" (Romans 8:37).

The issue is, How can that victory be achieved? The godliness of our lives is obviously quite dependent upon a proper answer.

THE WAY OF VICTORY

John deals with this issue in his first epistle also, stating, "This is the victory that has overcome the world — our faith" (1 John 5:4). John declares that the way of victory is the *way of faith.* It surely does not lie in our own self-effort or self-determination no matter how we may strive (Romans 7:18). Most have learned that in our own strength we are powerless against some if not many temptations. John tells us that victory comes through faith. Paul presents the same idea when he states, "In addition to all, taking up the shield of faith with which you will be able to extinguish all the flaming missiles of the evil one" (Ephesians 6:16). Faith is the victory!

It is important, however, to realize that faith must have an object. It will not do simply to say, "Have faith!" Genuine faith always has its foundation in truth: the Lord Himself and His truth. So it is in the matter of victory over sin by faith. In what reality then are we to place our faith? Let it be crystal clear; faith is always to be placed in the living Word of God, Jesus Christ Himself, and the truth of our Lord expressed in the Bible. In finding victory over sin, the same principle applies. What then is the truth of Scripture that points us to Christ where we rest in faith? The following rather lengthy passage is the answer. It bears a careful reading. Paul said,

> What shall we say then? Are we to continue in sin that grace might increase? May it never be! How shall we who died to sin still live in it? Or do you not know that all of us who have been baptized into Christ Jesus have been baptized into His death? Therefore we have been buried with Him through baptism into death, in order that as Christ was raised from the dead through the glory of the Father, so we too might walk in newness of life. For if we have become united with Him in the likeness of His death, certainly we shall be also in the likeness of His resurrection, knowing this, that our old self was crucified wih Him, that our body of sin might be done away with, that we should no longer be slaves to sin; for he who has died is freed from sin. Now if we have died with Christ, we believe that we shall also live with Him, knowing that Christ, having been raised from the dead, is never to die again; death no longer is master over Him. For the death that He died, He died to sin, once for all; but the life that He lives, He lives to God. Even so consider yourselves to be dead to sin, but alive to God in Christ Jesus. Therefore do not let sin reign in your mortal body that you should obey its lusts; and do not go on presenting the members of your body to sin as instruments of unrighteousness; but present yourselves to God as those alive from the dead, and your members as instruments of righteousness to God. For sin shall not be master over you, for you are not under law, but under grace. (Romans 6:1-14)

Can you see the impact of what Paul is saying? He states that if one is dead he is free from sin. That makes sense. There will be no sin in heaven. But if we are dead we will be of no value to Christ's service here on earth. That is also logical. If we could only be dead and alive at the same time that would solve our dilemma. But that is quite unthinkable — or is it? Right here Paul makes a startling statement. He says that because of our *union with Christ*, whereby we have been made one with Him, we have shared in our Lord's death on the cross. We are to understand that we have actually died with Christ to sin because we are "in Christ." In a spiritual sense — yet in a very real way — when Christ died on the cross, we died with Him. When He gained the victory by His blood, we shared in that victory by death. The rationality behind this is that God always sees us as *in Him*. (The concept of "in Christ" is the key to Pauline theology).

Therefore, what our Lord experienced, we have experienced. So we are already dead because He died. And as a result we are free from sin's dominion. It is no longer our master; our "old man" has been crucified with Christ (Galatians 2:20). Futhermore, not only have we died with Christ and shared in that experience of death, but because we are *in Him* we have also been spiritually resurrected with Him. We live because He lives. We are born again. We are now animated by the resurrected life of our Lord in the person of His Holy Spirit. Can sin thus dominate us? It absolutely cannot! We are dead to it and alive to God.

We must recognize that this truth does not appeal to one's mere rational logic. It is most difficult to realize these truths as we look at ourselves. Yet, God says it is true, and by faith we accept it. Actually, it is only faith that can grasp this tremendous reality. *But there lies victory*. As one author has pointedly expressed it,

> When Christ died on the cross to sin, we were identified with Him in that death to sin. That is we died *with* Him. By our union with Him in His death, we were freed from the penalty of sin and emancipated from the power of sin. All our sanctification therefore must be traced to, and rests upon, the atoning sacrifice of our Lord Jesus Christ. The cross of Christ is the efficient cause of deliverance from the power of sin. Freedom from the dominion of sin is a blessing we may claim by faith, just as we accept pardon.[2] (Italics added)

Here is how this principle works in one's everyday experience. Let us say we are met by one of our old temptations.

2. Steven Barabas, *So Great Salvation* (New York: Revell), pp. 88-89.

We have striven to overcome it, but with little success. We are sincere in wanting to live totally for Jesus Christ, but we seem to fail so often. Now, however, we realize our union with Christ in His death and resurrection and that by faith in Jesus Christ that identifies us with Him, and we say, "This sin has no more power over me; I am dead to it." Then in faith we look to God alone for the victory (faith is always essentially in His person) and Christ's resurrected life (the Holy Spirit) within us works complete victory over the temptation. Christ Himself, by His Spirit, is our victory. We have the Victor within. Faith releases the Holy Spirit in us. Assurance in the fact of our death to sin and a vital look of faith to God appropriating our position in Christ is the answer. You cannot separate faith or assurance in God's truth from vital faith in God *Himself*. They are two sides of the same coin.

Thus we live in a new freedom never before experienced. The battle — the "willing" aspect — of sin is not to fight sin and temptation *directly*. The battle is the will to stay on the ground of faith and appropriate victory. Faith is the victory that overcomes the world. Not only in eternity will we be delivered from the penalty and presence of sin, but now by faith we are saved from its power.

That is what it means to live a holy life, walking in actual fellowship with the living Christ, daily being cleansed when we err. By exercising constant faith in Him because of our identification with Him, we find Him achieving victory and appropriating His victory to us. That is what will make us powerful witnesses.

THE POWER OF THE HOLY SPIRIT

The work of the Holy Spirit must be recognized to be an effective witness. If this be true, what then is the scriptural principle of our relationship to the Spirit of God? First, it should be made clear that *all* believers are indwelt by the Holy Spirit and sealed by His stamp. That is clear from the New Testament. But there is another issue: the power issue. A believer is not to be merely a possessor of the spirit, he is to be *filled* with the spirit. Ephesians 5:18 says, "And do not get drunk with wine, for that is dissipation, but be filled with the Spirit."

But how does one experience the fullness of the Spirit and walk in His daily anointing? First, one must confess and forsake all known sins (we can hardly confess *unknown* sin; we are not calling for "sinless perfection"). The heart, as much as we can know it, must be cleansed by the blood of Christ (1 John 1:9). This principle has already been amply discussed. Then, one must surrender without reservation to Jesus Christ as Lord of life (Romans 12:1-2). Remember what the prophet Samuel told rebellious King Saul: "Behold, to obey is better than sacrifice, and to heed than the fat of rams" (1 Samuel 15:22). God requires our absolute obedience. We must be yielded vessels before we can become filled vessels.

Finally, one should pray and simply trust God to do the work of filling (Luke 11:13). It is actually that simple. Yet, it is most profound. The very moment we confess all known sins, surrender totally to Christ, and trust God to fill us with His Spirit, He will surely meet our need and we will become Spirit-filled Christians.

As implied, there is a definite relationship between being filled with the Spirit and daily walking with Christ as discussed earlier. We must recognize that being filled with the Spirit is not a once-for-all experience; neither is it something that brings one into a state of sinless perfection. Let that be very clear. Further, there is not one particular gift of the Spirit one must receive to know he or she is filled. God gives spiritual gifts as He chooses. It is not necessarily even an emotional experience. The point is, being filled with the Spirit is an experience that we need *each day*. That is where the scriptural emphasis lies. As someone has said, we are "leaky vessels," and we thus need to be "refilled" regularly. This is why Paul says in Ephesians 5:18 (literally), "*Continue* to be filled with the Spirit" (italics added). Being filled with the spirit is a *continuing experience*.

Thus the relationship begins to emerge: As we walk with Christ in faith, surrender, and confession, we daily come to Him as empty vessels to a full fountain, to be made full and running over with His Spirit. The indwelling Holy Spirit will fill us with His presence and power. But if we fail to walk with Christ, through rebellion or refusal to confess our sins or live by faith, we will surely fail to come to Him for the divine infilling of His Holy Spirit, and we are thus impotent in His service and we lose the conscious glow of Christ's presence.

To walk with God, therefore, is to walk in the continual infilling of His power as well as in constant cleansing. It is like "spiritual breathing": we exhale by confession and inhale by being filled with the Spirit. Obviously, when this is one's perpetual experience, he or she is bound to exemplify the power of a holy life and the dynamic of the Holy Spirit for witnessing and all Christian service.

THE POWER OF A HOLY PASSION

David Brainerd, missionary to the American Indians, said, "I cared not where or how I lived or what hardships I went through so that I could but gain souls for Christ. While I was asleep I dreamed of these things, and when I awoke the first thing I thought of was this great work. All of my desire was for the conversion of the heathen and all my hope was in God."

In a similar spirit, Thomas Chalmers prayed, "Recall the twenty-one years of my service; give me back its shipwreck, give me its standings in the face of death, give me it surrounded by fierce savages with spears and clubs, give it back to me with clubs knocking me down, give all this back to me, and I will be your missionary still."

That is the attitude God honors. And that is the kind of passion that communicates to people. John Wesley is reported to have said, "Get on fire for God and people will come and watch you burn." The passion for people that the Holy Spirit imparts is not to be quenched. God desires His "evangelists" to be burdened, concerned, enthusiastic, and zealous to spread the good news to the millions who desperately need to hear the message. The Holy Spirit will instill this attitude as we seek His strength, wisdom, and compassion.

THE POWER OF PRAYER

Prayer is a tremendous resource of power. Only a word or two about it will be said here. Let it simply be said, but strongly emphasized, that prayer is *essential* to spiritual power in one's life. Every great spiritual movement has been conceived, born, and matured in intercession. All effective witnessing to skeptics or anyone else has to be saturated with prayer. Through the years of God's dealings, prayer has been the key that opens the treasure house of God's power. So pray!

Perhaps the best way to complete this epilogue would be with a prayer. The following prayer may help express your desire for all you need to be an effective witness for Christ as you respond to the skeptic.

Father,

Help us to do Your work on earth, whatever it be, whenever we can, wherever we are.

Help us to befriend the lonely, comfort the hurting, feed the hungry, and reach those without Christ.

Help us as Christians to accept our God-given responsibility to witness in spirit and truth.

Help us to forever realize that though we may study and serve, preach and teach, we are nothing without love and the power of your Holy Spirit.

Help us always to listen attentively, speak carefully, witness willingly, and give sacrificially.

As Jesus did, in whose Name we pray. Amen.